COMPLETE

Charcuterie

COMPLETE
Charcuterie

OVER 200 CONTEMPORARY
RECIPES & SPREADS
FOR EASY ENTERTAINING

CIDER MILL PRESS

BOOK PUBLISHERS

CONTENTS

Introduction 7

Breads & Crackers 12

Dips, Spreads & Condiments 94

Land to Sea 184

Dumplings & Other Decadent Bites 240

Return to the Garden 302

Something Sweet 384

Index 441

INTRODUCTION

Mastering the art of charcuterie relies on the same secret as succeeding at the art of life: it's all about relationships.

One can have all the talent in the world, but if they can't communicate with anyone, there's an extremely good chance that their gifts will never receive their due. With charcuterie, you can be an ace in the kitchen, have access to extraordinary cheese and wine shops, have the keen curatorial eye needed to put together an appealing board, but if you don't understand what pairs well with what, your boards are going to fall far short of your and everyone else's expectations.

It is not enough to be good at one or two of these things, you need to be good at all of them.

This book is not going to get you all the way there—to be truthful, only the experience of going through the process, seeing what works and what does not, can do that. But it will help you shore up whatever area you are lacking in, providing the positive results one needs to keep plugging away and improving. Looking to expand your repertoire? A host of innovative and classic recipes plucked from cuisines around the globe make it easy to keep things fresh. Need some help making your boards visually appealing? A series of beautifully composed boards are sprinkled throughout the book to provide instruction and inspiration. Unsure what other items that imported spicy salami will be best beside? Each recipe comes with a number of suggested pairings that, even if you decide to cut against them, will at least provide some direction.

That direction is key, because within the narrow boundaries of a serving board lie infinite possibilities. Whatever strikes one as worthy of celebrating—from freshly baked bread to breakfast foods and decadent desserts—can work as part of a spread. Such freedom is exciting, but also makes it difficult to know exactly how to proceed if one is going to fulfill this limitless promise. When one is faced with a blank board, it is easy for questions and doubts to arise.

Questions are not in themselves bad. But if they come too quickly, before any decisions have been made, it's easy to become overwhelmed. Once one item has been chosen, a partner is sure to arise. Decide whether you want to cut smartly against this pairing or roll with it in terms of taste or texture, pair this new piece with something harmonious, and you're well on your way.

But how does one know what to start with? If you take a step back, we're willing to bet that this answer is standing right before you, screaming itself hoarse trying to get your attention. Perhaps the tomatoes in the garden have just reached their peak. Maybe the farm stand down the road has a new, intriguing spread on offer. Take a step outside your front door—is the day calling for oysters, mignonette sauce, and a bottle of Picpoul? For rich stout, soft pretzels, mustard, and bratwurst? Paying attention to signals such as these will pay huge dividends on the final board.

Once you have that initial item set, the rest gets easier. Do your best to have a balance of sweet, savory, tart, earthy and spicy flavors and a variety of textures, from crispy and chewy to creamy, on your charcuterie boards. But don't become so obsessed with striking this balance that you end up losing the plot entirely.

One can compose a beautiful, delicious platter by doing little more than pushing a cart around the grocery store, loading it up with cheeses, cured meats, and olives, unwrapping, and arranging your purchases on a board. But in truth there is something unwelcoming about a strictly store-bought board, a lack of personal touch that, even if everything is delicious, makes the spread feel a little less special.

Instead, it's good to have a mix of purchased items and homemade goods, which make it easy to add variety and something unique to each board. The more personal a board feels, the more in tune with a person and a place, the happier those around it will be, and the better the resulting conversations. Which is what the serving board is really all about, right?

BREADS & CRACKERS

For many of the offerings in this chapter, it's tempting to turn to one of the talented artisans who have elected to devote their lives to the famously tricky work of baking. But committing to make them at home will lend your charcuterie boards a personal touch, and provide you with the confidence to become a true master.

FETA & HERB
Quickbread

YIELD: 1 LOAF / **ACTIVE TIME:** 10 MINUTES / **TOTAL TIME:** 1 HOUR

INGREDIENTS

½ cup finely chopped fresh basil

½ cup finely chopped fresh chives

Unsalted butter, as needed

2 tablespoons sesame seeds

1¼ cups all-purpose flour

1 tablespoon baking powder

3 large organic eggs

¼ cup extra-virgin olive oil

½ cup plain yogurt, plus
2 tablespoons

½ teaspoon fine sea salt

½ teaspoon black pepper

7 oz. feta cheese

1   Preheat the oven to 350°F. Combine the basil and chives in a small bowl and set the mixture aside. Coat a 9 x 5–inch loaf pan with butter and sprinkle half of the sesame seeds onto the bottom and sides, shaking the pan to coat.

2   Combine the flour and baking powder in a bowl. In a separate bowl, whisk together the eggs, oil, yogurt, salt, and pepper. Stir in the feta and herb mixture. Fold the flour mixture into the egg mixture. Be careful not to overmix the batter—it is fine if a few lumps remain.

3   Pour the batter into the prepared pan. Level the surface with a spatula and sprinkle the remaining sesame seeds on top. Bake until the top is golden and a knife inserted into the center comes out clean, 40 to 50 minutes.

4   Remove the bread from the oven and let it cool in the pan for a few minutes. Run a knife around the edges of the pan to loosen the bread and then transfer it to a wire rack. Let the bread cool completely before enjoying.

PAIRS WELL WITH: CREAMY SPREADS & DIPS, CURED MEATS, SPRING-THEMED BOARDS

SOURDOUGH
Starter

YIELD: 2 CUPS / **ACTIVE TIME:** 2 HOURS / **TOTAL TIME:** 2 WEEKS

INGREDIENTS

1 cup water, at room temperature, plus more daily

2 cups all-purpose flour, plus more daily

1 Place the water and flour in a large jar (the jar should be at least 1 quart). Combine the ingredients by hand, cover the jar, and let stand in a sunny spot at room temperature for 24 hours.

2 Place 1 cup of the starter in a bowl, add 1 cup water and 2 cups flour, and stir until thoroughly combined. Discard the remainder of the starter. Place the new mixture back in the jar and let it sit at room temperature for 24 hours. Repeat this process every day until you notice bubbles forming in the starter. This should take approximately 2 weeks.

3 Once the starter begins to bubble, it can be used in recipes. The starter can be stored at room temperature or in the refrigerator. If the starter is kept at room temperature it must be fed once a day; if the starter is refrigerated it can be fed every 3 days. The starter can be frozen for up to a month without feeding.

4 To feed the starter, place 1 cup of the starter in a bowl, add 1 cup flour and 1 cup water, and work the mixture with your hands until combined. Discard the remainder of the starter. It is recommended that you feed the starter 6 to 8 hours before making bread.

SOURDOUGH
Bread

YIELD: 1 BOULE / **ACTIVE TIME:** 1 HOUR AND 30 MINUTES / **TOTAL TIME:** 24 HOURS

INGREDIENTS

1 cup water, at room temperature

3⅓ cups bread flour, plus more as needed

⅓ cup whole wheat flour

1 cup Sourdough Starter (see page 16)

2 teaspoons kosher salt

1 Place the water and flours in the work bowl of a stand mixer fitted with the dough hook and work the mixture at low speed for 6 minutes. Remove the bowl from the mixer and cover it with plastic wrap. Let the dough sit at room temperature for 1 hour to allow the dough to autolyse.

2 Place the work bowl back on the mixer and add the starter and salt. Knead the mixture at low speed until the dough starts to come together, about 2 minutes. Increase the speed to medium and knead until the dough is elastic and pulls away from the side of the bowl.

3 Dust a 9-inch banneton (proofing basket) with flour. Shape the dough into a ball and place it in the proofing basket, seam side down. Cover the bread with plastic wrap and let it sit on the counter for 2 hours.

4 Place the basket in the refrigerator and let it rest overnight.

5 Preheat the oven to 450°F and place a baking stone on a rack positioned in the middle.

6 Dust a peel with flour and gently turn the bread onto the peel so that the seam is facing up.

7 With a very sharp knife, carefully score the dough just off center. Make sure the knife is at a 45-degree angle to the dough.

8 Gently slide the sourdough onto the baking stone. Spray the oven with 5 spritzes of water and bake the bread for 20 minutes.

9 Open the oven, spray the oven with 5 more spritzes, and bake until the crust is golden brown, about 20 minutes. The internal temperature of the bread should be at minimum 210°F. Remove the bread from the oven, place it on a wire rack, and let it cool completely before slicing.

PAIRS WELL WITH: AUTUMN-THEMED BOARDS, CURED MEATS, VEGETABLE-BASED SPREADS

BLACK SESAME
Sourdough Bread

YIELD: 1 BOULE / ACTIVE TIME: 1 HOUR AND 30 MINUTES / TOTAL TIME: 24 HOURS

INGREDIENTS

1 cup water, at room temperature

3⅓ cups bread flour, plus more as needed

⅓ cup whole wheat flour

½ cup black tahini paste

1 cup Sourdough Starter (see page 16)

2 teaspoons kosher salt

1 cup black sesame seeds

1 Place the water and flours in the work bowl of a stand mixer fitted with the dough hook and work the mixture at low speed for 6 minutes. Remove the bowl from the mixer and cover it with plastic wrap. Let the dough sit at room temperature for 1 hour to allow the dough to autolyse.

2 Place the work bowl back on the mixer and add the black tahini paste, starter, and salt. Knead the mixture at low speed until the dough starts to come together, about 2 minutes. Increase the speed to medium and knead until the dough is elastic and pulls away from the side of the bowl.

3 Place the sesame seeds on a plate. Shape the dough into a ball and spray the seam side with water. Roll the top of the dough in the sesame seeds until coated.

4 Dust a 9-inch banneton (proofing basket) with flour. Place the dough in the proofing basket, seeded side down. Cover the bread with plastic wrap and let it sit on the counter for 2 hours.

5 Place the basket in the refrigerator and let it rest overnight.

6 Preheat the oven to 450°F and place a baking stone on a rack positioned in the middle.

7 Dust a peel with flour and gently turn the bread onto the peel so that the seeded side is facing up.

8 With a very sharp knife, carefully score the dough just off center. Make sure the knife is at a 45-degree angle to the dough.

9 Gently slide the sourdough onto the baking stone. Spray the oven with 5 spritzes of water and bake the bread for 20 minutes.

10 Open the oven, spray the oven with 5 more spritzes, and bake until the crust is golden brown, about 20 minutes. The internal temperature of the bread should be at minimum 210°F. Remove the bread from the oven, place it on a wire rack, and let it cool completely before slicing.

PAIRS WELL WITH: LEMON RICOTTA (SEE PAGE 281), HONEYCOMB, SALAMI

BLUE PEA FLOWER
Sourdough Bread

YIELD: 1 BOULE / **ACTIVE TIME:** 1 HOUR AND 30 MINUTES / **TOTAL TIME:** 24 HOURS

INGREDIENTS

1 cup water, at room temperature

3⅓ cups bread flour, plus more as needed

⅓ cup whole wheat flour

¼ cup blue pea flower powder

1 cup Sourdough Starter (see page 16)

2 teaspoons kosher salt

1. Place the water, flours, and blue pea flower powder in the work bowl of a stand mixer fitted with the dough hook and work the mixture at low speed for 6 minutes. Remove the bowl from the mixer and cover it with plastic wrap. Let the dough sit at room temperature for 1 hour to allow the dough to autolyse.

2. Place the work bowl back on the mixer and add the starter and salt. Knead the mixture at low speed until the dough starts to come together, about 2 minutes. Increase the speed to medium and knead until the dough is elastic and pulls away from the side of the bowl.

3. Shape the dough into a ball and spray the seam side with water. Dust a 9-inch banneton (proofing basket) with flour. Place the dough in the proofing basket, seam side down. Cover the bread with plastic wrap and let it sit on the counter for 2 hours.

4. Place the basket in the refrigerator and let it rest overnight.

5. Preheat the oven to 450°F and place a baking stone on a rack positioned in the middle.

6. Dust a peel with flour and gently turn the bread onto the peel so that the seam is facing up.

7. With a very sharp knife, carefully score the dough just off center. Make sure the knife is at a 45-degree angle to the dough.

8. Gently slide the sourdough onto the baking stone. Spray the oven with 5 spritzes of water and bake the bread for 20 minutes.

9. Open the oven, spray the oven with 5 more spritzes, and bake until the crust is golden brown, about 20 minutes. The internal temperature of the bread should be at minimum 210°F.

PAIRS WELL WITH: VEGETABLE SPREADS, TART CONDIMENTS, SPRING- & SUMMER-THEMED BOARDS

BAGUETTES

YIELD: 2 BAGUETTES / **ACTIVE TIME:** 1 HOUR AND 30 MINUTES / **TOTAL TIME:** 24 HOURS

INGREDIENTS

5 oz. water

11½ oz. bread flour, plus more as needed

½ oz. whole wheat flour

1 teaspoon sugar

1 cup Sourdough Starter (see page 16)

1 tablespoon kosher salt

1 Place the water, flours, and sugar in the work bowl of a stand mixer fitted with the dough hook and work the mixture at low speed for 6 minutes. Remove the bowl from the mixer and cover it with plastic wrap. Let the dough sit at room temperature for 1 hour to allow the dough to autolyse.

2 Place the work bowl back on the mixer and add the starter and salt. Knead the mixture at low speed until the dough starts to come together, about 2 minutes. Increase the speed to medium and knead until the dough is elastic and pulls away from the side of the bowl.

3 Shape the dough into a ball and spray the seam side with water. Dust a 9-inch banneton (proofing basket) with flour. Place the dough in the proofing basket, seam side down. Cover the bread with plastic wrap and let it sit on the counter for 2 hours.

4 Place the dough on a flour-dusted work surface, divide it in half, and shape each piece into a ball. Cover the dough with a moist linen towel and let it sit on the counter for 15 minutes.

5 Punch down the pieces of dough until they are rough ovals. Working with one piece at a time, take the side closest to you and roll it away from you. Starting halfway up, fold in the corners and roll the dough into a rough baguette shape.

6 Place both hands over one piece of dough. Gently roll the dough while moving your hands back and forth over it and gently pressing down until it is about 16 inches long. Repeat with the other piece of dough.

7 Place the baguettes on a baguette pan, cover with plastic wrap, and chill them in the refrigerator overnight.

8 Remove the baguettes from the refrigerator, place the pan in a naturally warm spot, and let it sit for 2 hours.

9 Preheat the oven to 450°F.

10 Using a very sharp knife, cut four slits at a 45-degree angle along the length of each baguette.

11 Place the baguettes in the oven, spray the oven with 5 spritzes of water, and bake until the baguettes are a deep golden brown, 20 to 30 minutes.

12 Remove the baguettes from the oven, place them on a wire rack, and let them cool slightly before slicing.

PAIRS WELL WITH: BUTTERY CHEESES, HERB-BASED CONDIMENTS, CURED MEATS

CIABATTA

YIELD: 1 LOAF / **ACTIVE TIME:** 1 HOUR / **TOTAL TIME:** 24 HOURS

INGREDIENTS

For the Poolish

7½ oz. lukewarm water (90°F)

¼ teaspoon active dry yeast

2¼ cups all-purpose flour

For the Dough

¾ cup water

¾ teaspoon active dry yeast

2 teaspoons honey

12½ oz. bread flour, plus more as needed

2¼ teaspoons kosher salt

1 To prepare the poolish, place all the ingredients in a mixing bowl and whisk to combine. Cover the bowl with a linen towel and let it sit at room temperature overnight.

2 To begin preparations for the dough, place the poolish in the work bowl of a stand mixer fitted with the dough hook. Add the water, yeast, and honey and whisk to combine. Add the flour and work the mixture on low for 1 minute. Raise the speed to medium and knead the mixture for 5 minutes. Turn off the mixer and let it rest for 5 minutes.

3 Add the salt and knead the mixture on low for 1 minute. Raise the speed to medium and knead the dough until it is very well developed and starts to pull away from the side of the work bowl, about 8 minutes.

4 Spray a 13 x 9–inch baking pan with nonstick cooking spray. Place the dough in the pan, cover it with plastic wrap, and let it rise for 45 minutes.

5 Take one end of the dough and fold a third of it over the center of the dough. Take the other end of the dough and fold over this third. Turn the pan 90 degrees and gently flip the dough over so that the fresh fold is facing down. Cover the pan and let it rise for 45 minutes. After 45 minutes, repeat the folding and resting process twice more.

6 Line a baking sheet with parchment paper. Place the dough on a flour-dusted work surface and repeat the folding process used in Step 5. Place the dough on the baking sheet and let it rise for 45 minutes.

7 Preheat the oven to 400°F.

8 Place the bread in the oven and spray the oven generously with water to increase the humidity in the oven. Bake for 10 minutes, open the oven, and generously spray it with water. Bake for another 10 minutes, open the oven, and spray it generously with water one last time.

9 Close the oven and let the ciabatta bake until golden brown and crispy, about 20 minutes. The internal temperature should be 210°F.

10 Remove the ciabatta from the oven, place it on a wire rack, and let it cool before enjoying.

PAIRS WELL WITH: ANTIPASTO, HERB-BASED CONDIMENTS, SHARP & NUTTY CHEESES

FOCACCIA

YIELD: 18 X 13–INCH FOCACCIA / **ACTIVE TIME:** 45 MINUTES / **TOTAL TIME:** 4 HOURS

INGREDIENTS

For the Poolish

3¼ cups water

2 tablespoons active dry yeast

½ cup sugar

½ cup extra-virgin olive oil, plus 2 tablespoons

For the Dough

28 oz. bread flour

20 oz. all-purpose flour

2 tablespoons finely chopped fresh rosemary

1 tablespoon finely chopped fresh thyme

2 tablespoons finely chopped fresh basil

3 tablespoons kosher salt

1½ teaspoons black pepper

1½ cups extra-virgin olive oil, plus more as needed

1 cup freshly shaved Parmesan cheese

1 To prepare the poolish, place all the ingredients in a mixing bowl and whisk to combine. Cover the bowl with a linen towel and let it sit at room temperature for 30 minutes.

2 To begin preparations for the dough, place the poolish in the work bowl of a stand mixer fitted with the dough hook. Add all the remaining ingredients, except for the olive oil and Parmesan, and work the mixture on low for 1 minute. Raise the speed to medium and knead the mixture until it comes together as a smooth dough, about 5 minutes. Cover the bowl with a linen towel and let the dough rise until it has doubled in size.

3 Preheat the oven to 350°F.

4 Coat an 18 x 13–inch sheet pan with olive oil and place the dough on the pan. Use your fingers to gradually stretch the dough until it fills the entire pan and is as even as possible. If the dough is difficult to stretch, let it rest for 10 minutes before resuming.

5 Cover the dough with plastic wrap and let it rise at room temperature until it has doubled in size.

6 Use your fingertips to gently press down on the dough and make dimples all over it. The dimples should go about halfway down. Drizzle about 1 cup of olive oil over the focaccia and sprinkle the Parmesan on top.

7 Place the focaccia in the oven and bake until it is a light golden brown, 20 to 30 minutes.

8 Remove the focaccia from the oven and brush it generously with olive oil. Let it cool slightly before slicing and serving.

BRIOCHE

YIELD: 2 LOAVES / **ACTIVE TIME:** 45 MINUTES / **TOTAL TIME:** 4 HOURS

INGREDIENTS

For the Sponge

½ cup milk, warmed

4½ teaspoons active dry yeast

2 tablespoons honey

4 oz. bread flour

For the Dough

5 eggs, 1 beaten

2 oz. sugar

1 lb. bread flour

2 teaspoons kosher salt

4 oz. unsalted butter, softened

1   To prepare the sponge, place all the ingredients in the work bowl of a stand mixer. Cover with plastic wrap and let the mixture sit until it starts to bubble, about 30 minutes.

2   To begin preparations for the dough, add the 4 unbeaten eggs to the sponge and whisk until incorporated.

3   Add the sugar, flour, and salt, fit the mixer with the dough hook, and knead the mixture on low speed for 5 minutes.

4   Over the course of 2 minutes, add the butter a little at a time with the mixer running. When all the butter has been added, knead the mixture on low for 5 minutes.

5   Raise the speed to medium and knead the dough until it begins to pull away from the side of the work bowl, about 6 minutes. Cover the bowl with a kitchen towel, place the dough in a naturally warm spot, and let it rise until it has doubled in size, about 1 hour.

6   Preheat the oven to 350°F. Coat two 8 x 4–inch loaf pans with nonstick cooking spray.

7   Divide the dough into two equal pieces and flatten each one into a rectangle the width of a loaf pan. Tuck in the sides to form the dough into loaf shapes and place one in each pan, seam side down.

8   Cover the pans with plastic wrap and let the dough rise until it has crested over the tops of the pans.

9   Brush the loaves with the beaten egg, place them in the oven, and bake until golden brown, 35 to 45 minutes. The loaves should reach an internal temperature of 200°F.

10 Remove from the oven, place the pans on a wire rack, and let them cool before enjoying.

PAIRS WELL WITH: JAM, HONEYCOMB, BREAKFAST & BRUNCH BOARDS

CHALLAH

YIELD: 1 LOAF / **ACTIVE TIME:** 1 HOUR / **TOTAL TIME:** 5 HOURS

1   Place the water and yeast in the work bowl of a stand mixer and gently whisk to combine. Let the mixture sit until it starts to foam, about 10 minutes.

2   Fit the mixer with the dough hook, add the 3 unbeaten eggs, oil, flour, sugar, and salt to the work bowl, and work the mixture on low until it comes together as a dough, about 2 minutes.

3   Raise the speed to medium and knead until the dough becomes elastic and starts to pull away from the side of the bowl, about 6 minutes.

4   Cover the mixing bowl with a kitchen towel, place it in a naturally warm spot, and let the dough rise until it has doubled in size.

5   Place the dough on a flour-dusted work surface and punch it down. Divide the dough into four pieces that are each 12.7 oz. Shape the pieces into ovals, cover with linen towels, and let them rest for 15 to 30 minutes.

6   Preheat the oven to 350°F. Line a baking sheet with parchment paper.

7   Using the palms of your hands, gently roll the dough into strands that are about 2 feet long.

8   Take the strands and fan them out so that one end of each of them is touching. Press down on the ends where they are touching. Take the right-most strand (Strand 1) and cross it over to the left so that it is horizontal. Take the left-most strand (Strand 2) and cross it over to the right so that it is horizontal.

9   Move Strand 1 between the two strands that have yet to move. Move the strand to the right of Strand 1 to the left so that it is horizontal. This will be known as Strand 3.

10   Move Strand 2 between Strand 1 and Strand 4. Move strand 4 to the right so that it is horizontal.

11   Repeat moving the horizontal strands to the middle and replacing them with the opposite, outer strands until the entire loaf is braided. Pinch the ends of the loaf together and tuck them under the bread.

12   Brush the dough with the beaten egg. If you want to top the bread with poppy seeds, sesame seeds, or herbs, now is the time to sprinkle them over the top.

13   Place the bread in the oven and bake it until golden brown, about 30 minutes. The cooked challah should have an internal temperature of 210°F.

14   Remove the challah from the oven, place it on a wire rack, and let it cool completely before enjoying.

PAIRS WELL WITH: JAM, CREAMY SPREADS, SMOKED MEATS

INGREDIENTS

1½ cups lukewarm water (90°F)

1 tablespoon active dry yeast, plus 2 teaspoons

4 eggs, 1 beaten

¼ cup extra-virgin olive oil

7 cups bread flour, plus more as needed

¼ cup sugar

1½ tablespoons kosher salt

HARVEST
Loaf

YIELD: 1 LOAF / ACTIVE TIME: 45 MINUTES / TOTAL TIME: 4 HOURS

INGREDIENTS

6 oz. lukewarm water (90°F)

1 tablespoon active dry yeast

2 eggs, 1 beaten

1 egg yolk

1 oz. extra-virgin olive oil

1 oz. sugar

15 oz. bread flour, plus more as needed

1 teaspoon ground cloves

1 tablespoon cinnamon

1 cup dried cranberries

½ cup pumpkin seeds, toasted

2 teaspoons kosher salt

1 Place the water in the work bowl of a stand mixer. Sprinkle the yeast over the water, gently whisk, and let the mixture sit for 10 minutes.

2 Add the unbeaten egg, egg yolk, olive oil, and sugar and fit the mixer with the dough hook. Add the flour, cloves, cinnamon, cranberries, pumpkin seeds, and salt and work the mixture on low speed until it just starts to come together as a dough, about 1 minute.

3 Raise the speed to medium and work the dough until it comes away clean from the side of the work bowl and is elastic, about 6 minutes.

4 Spray a mixing bowl with nonstick cooking spray. Transfer the dough to a flour-dusted work surface and knead it until it is extensible. Shape the dough into a ball, place it in the bowl, and cover the bowl with a kitchen towel. Place the dough in a naturally warm spot and let it rise until doubled in size, 1 to 2 hours.

5 Preheat the oven to 350°F. Spray an 8 x 4–inch loaf pan with nonstick cooking spray.

6 Place the dough on a flour-dusted work surface and roll it into a tight round. Tuck the ends in toward the center and place the dough in the loaf pan, seam side down. Cover the dough with plastic wrap, place it in a naturally warm spot, and let it rise until doubled in size.

7 Brush the dough with the beaten egg. Using a very sharp knife, cut a seam that runs the length of the bread on top. Place the dough in the oven and bake the bread until it is golden brown, 35 to 45 minutes. The internal temperature of the bread should be 200°F.

8 Remove the bread from the oven, place it on a cooling rack, and let it cool completely before slicing.

PAIRS WELL WITH: FRUIT, SOFT & BUTTERY CHEESES, AUTUMN-THEMED BOARDS

FOUGASSE

YIELD: 1 LOAF / **ACTIVE TIME:** 30 MINUTES / **TOTAL TIME:** 3 HOURS

INGREDIENTS

9 oz. water

2½ teaspoons active dry yeast

3 tablespoons extra-virgin olive oil, plus more as needed

15 oz. bread flour, plus more as needed

1 tablespoon dried basil, plus 1 teaspoon

2 garlic cloves, minced

1 tablespoon kosher salt

¼ cup freshly shaved Parmesan cheese

1 In the work bowl of a stand mixer fitted with the paddle attachment, add the water and yeast, gently whisk to combine, and let the mixture sit for 10 minutes.

2 Add the oil, flour, basil, garlic, and salt and work the mixture on low for 1 minute. Raise the speed to medium and work the mixture until it comes together as a smooth dough, about 5 minutes.

3 Remove the dough from the work bowl, place it on a flour-dusted work surface, and knead it until it is elastic. Shape the dough into a ball, return it to the work bowl, and cover it with plastic wrap. Place the dough in a naturally warm spot and let it rise until it has doubled in size.

4 Turn the dough out onto a flour-dusted surface. Lightly flour the top of the dough. Using a rolling pin, roll the dough out by starting in the middle of the dough and rolling toward you until it is an approximately 10 x 6–inch oval.

5 Preheat the oven to 350°F. Coat an 18 x 13–inch sheet pan with olive oil. Carefully place the dough in the center of the pan.

6 Using a pizza cutter, cut a lengthwise line in the center of the oval, leaving an inch uncut at each end so that the dough remains one piece. Make three small, angled slices to the left of the center cut. Do the same to the right of the center cut.

7 The bread should resemble a leaf. Lightly brush the dough with olive oil, cover the pan with plastic wrap, and let it rise until it has doubled in size.

8 Preheat the oven to 350°F.

9 Sprinkle the Parmesan over the bread, place it in the oven, and bake until it is golden brown, 20 to 30 minutes.

10 Remove the fougasse from the oven and brush it with more olive oil. Transfer it to a wire rack and let it cool completely before enjoying.

PAIRS WELL WITH: AUTUMN-THEMED BOARDS, CRUDITÉS, NUTTY CHEESES

BULKIE
Rolls

YIELD: 8 ROLLS / **ACTIVE TIME:** 45 MINUTES / **TOTAL TIME:** 4 HOURS

INGREDIENTS

6 oz. water

1½ teaspoons active dry yeast

2 eggs, 1 beaten

1 egg yolk

1 oz. extra-virgin olive oil

1 oz. sugar

15 oz. bread flour, plus more as needed

1 teaspoon kosher salt

1. Place the water, yeast, unbeaten egg, egg yolk, olive oil, and sugar in the work bowl of a stand mixer fitted with the dough hook and whisk to combine. Add the flour and salt and knead on low for 1 minute. Raise the speed to medium and knead the mixture until it comes together as a smooth dough and begins to pull away from the side of the work bowl, 6 to 8 minutes.

2. Coat a mixing bowl with nonstick cooking spray. Remove the dough from the work bowl, place it on a flour-dusted work surface, and shape it into a ball. Place the dough in the bowl, cover it with plastic wrap, place it in a naturally warm spot, and let it rise until doubled in size.

3. Line an 18 x 13–inch sheet pan with parchment paper. Place the dough on a flour-dusted work surface and divide it into 3.5-oz. portions. Roll the portions into tight balls. Place the balls on the pan, cover with plastic wrap, and place in a naturally warm spot. Let them rise until they have doubled in size.

4. Preheat the oven to 350°F.

5. Brush the balls with the beaten egg. Using a sharp knife, score an "X" on top of each ball.

6. Place the pan in the oven and bake until the rolls are golden brown, 20 to 25 minutes. The internal temperature of the rolls should be 190°F.

7. Remove from the oven, transfer the rolls to a wire rack, and let cool completely before enjoying.

PAIRS WELL WITH: COLD CUTS, ROASTED VEGETABLES

BROWN
Bread

YIELD: 1 LOAF / ACTIVE TIME: 15 MINUTES / TOTAL TIME: 1 HOUR

INGREDIENTS

11 oz. milk

½ cup molasses

2 tablespoons light brown sugar

5 oz. all-purpose flour

2½ oz. cornmeal

5 oz. whole wheat flour

2 teaspoons baking powder

¾ teaspoon baking soda

5 oz. raisins

1 Preheat the oven to 350°F. Coat an 8 x 4–inch loaf pan with nonstick cooking spray.

2 In the work bowl of a stand mixer fitted with the paddle attachment, combine the milk and molasses. Add the remaining ingredients and beat until the mixture comes together as a smooth batter, about 2 minutes.

3 Pour the batter into the loaf pan, place it in the oven, and bake until a cake tester inserted into the center comes out clean, 45 minutes to 1 hour.

4 Remove the bread from the oven and let the bread cool slightly. Remove it from the pan, place it on a cooling rack, and let it cool slightly before serving.

PAIRS WELL WITH: AUTUMN-THEMED BOARDS, CURED MEATS, TART SPREADS & CONDIMENTS

PÃO DE
Queijo

YIELD: 12 BUNS / **ACTIVE TIME:** 20 MINUTES / **TOTAL TIME:** 45 MINUTES

INGREDIENTS

9 oz. tapioca starch

1 cup milk

4 oz. unsalted butter

1 teaspoon kosher salt

2 eggs

1½ cups grated Parmesan cheese

1 Preheat the oven to 350°F. Line an 18 x 13–inch sheet pan with parchment paper. Place the tapioca starch in the work bowl of a stand mixer fitted with the paddle attachment.

2 Place the milk, butter, and salt in a small saucepan and warm over medium heat until the butter has melted and the mixture is simmering.

3 Turn the mixer on low and slowly pour the milk mixture into the work bowl. Raise the speed to medium and work the mixture until it has cooled considerably.

4 Add the eggs one at a time and knead to incorporate. Add the grated cheese and knead the mixture until incorporated.

5 Scoop 2-oz. portions of the dough onto the pan, making sure to leave enough space between them.

6 Place the pan in the oven and bake until the rolls are puffy and light golden brown, 15 to 20 minutes.

7 Remove from the oven and enjoy immediately.

PAIRS WELL WITH: CURED MEATS, PICKLED VEGETABLES, NUTTY CHEESES

GRISSINI
Sticks

YIELD: 24 STICKS / ACTIVE TIME: 30 MINUTES / TOTAL TIME: 3 HOURS

INGREDIENTS

4½ oz. milk

1 oz. water

2 teaspoons active dry yeast

1 oz. unsalted butter, melted

9 oz. all-purpose flour, plus more as needed

2 teaspoons kosher salt, plus more to taste

1 tablespoon dried oregano

Extra-virgin olive oil, as needed

1   Place the milk, water, and yeast in the work bowl of a stand mixer fitted with the dough hook, gently stir to combine, and let the mixture sit until it starts to foam, about 10 minutes.

2   Add the butter, flour, salt, and oregano and knead on low for 1 minute. Raise the speed to medium and knead the mixture until it comes together as a smooth dough and begins to pull away from the side of the work bowl, about 5 minutes.

3   Coat a mixing bowl with nonstick cooking spray. Remove the dough from the work bowl, place it on a flour-dusted work surface, and shape it into a ball. Place the dough in the bowl, cover it with plastic wrap, place it in a naturally warm spot, and let it rise until doubled in size.

4   Preheat the oven to 400°F.

5   Line two baking sheets with parchment paper. Place the dough on a flour-dusted work surface and divide it in half. Roll each piece out until it is ¼ inch thick and cut them into ⅛-inch-wide ribbons.

6   Place the ribbons on the baking sheets, brush them with olive oil, and sprinkle salt over them. Place them in the oven and bake until golden brown, 10 to 15 minutes.

7   Remove from the oven and let the grissini sticks cool slightly before enjoying.

PAIRS WELL WITH: NUTTY CHEESES, HERB-BASED CONDIMENTS, SPRING-THEMED BOARDS

WHOLE WHEAT
Crackers

YIELD: 40 CRACKERS / ACTIVE TIME: 20 MINUTES / TOTAL TIME: 45 MINUTES

INGREDIENTS

5½ oz. whole wheat flour, plus more as needed

1 oz. sugar

½ teaspoon kosher salt

4 tablespoons unsalted butter, chilled and cubed

2 oz. water

Extra-virgin olive oil, as needed

Maldon sea salt, for topping

1 Preheat the oven to 400°F. Line an 18 x 13–inch sheet pan with parchment paper. Place the flour, sugar, kosher salt, and butter in a food processor and pulse until combined and the butter has been reduced to pea-sized pieces.

2 While the food processor is running, add the water and blitz until incorporated.

3 Tip the mixture onto a lightly floured work surface and knead it until it comes together as a soft, smooth dough. Place the dough in a small bowl, cover it with plastic wrap, and let it rest for 10 minutes.

4 Place the dough on a flour-dusted work surface and divide it in half. Roll each half until it is ⅛ inch thick, brush with olive oil, and cut into 2-inch squares. Place them on the pan and sprinkle sea salt over them.

5 Place the pan in the oven and bake until the crackers are crispy and lightly golden brown, 8 to 10 minutes. Remove from the oven and let the crackers cool on the pan before enjoying.

PAIRS WELL WITH: VEGETABLE-BASED SPREADS, CHEESES, CURED & SMOKED MEATS, JAM

FETT'UNTA

YIELD: 4 SERVINGS / **ACTIVE TIME:** 10 MINUTES / **TOTAL TIME:** 30 MINUTES

INGREDIENTS

4 slices from loaf of crusty bread (each slice should be 1½ inches thick)

¾ cup quality extra-virgin olive oil, plus more as needed

1 garlic clove

Flaky sea salt, to taste

1 Preheat your gas or charcoal grill to high heat (500°F). Brush both sides of the bread generously with olive oil.

2 Place the bread on the grill and cook until crisp and browned on both sides, about 2 minutes per side.

3 Remove from heat, rub the garlic clove over one side of each piece, and pour 3 tablespoons of oil over each one. Sprinkle the salt over the top and serve.

PAIRS WELL WITH: ANTIPASTO, MILD CHEESES, ROASTED VEGETABLES

CROSTINI

YIELD: 6 SERVINGS / ACTIVE TIME: 15 MINUTES / TOTAL TIME: 30 MINUTES

INGREDIENTS

1 Baguette (see page 24), sliced

2 tablespoons extra-virgin olive oil, plus more to taste

Salt and pepper, to taste

1 Preheat the oven to 400°F. Brush the slices of baguette with the olive oil and place them on a baking sheet. Place in the oven and bake for 12 to 15 minutes, turning the slices over halfway through. When the slices are crispy and golden brown on both sides, remove the pan from the oven.

2 Top the crostini as desired, drizzle olive oil over them, and season with salt and pepper.

Note: There are limitless ways you can utilize these crostini. Those pictured feature ricotta and pea shoots, but you can top them with anything you like, or just serve them on the side and let people top them as they please.

PAIRS WELL WITH: CRUDITÉS, CREAMY CHEESES & SPREADS, CURED MEATS

TOAST
Points

YIELD: 4 SERVINGS / **ACTIVE TIME:** 5 MINUTES / **TOTAL TIME:** 25 MINUTES

INGREDIENTS

6 slices of bread

Extra-virgin olive oil, to taste

Salt and pepper, to taste

1   Preheat the oven to 350°F. Remove the crusts from the slices of bread and use a rolling pin to roll them flat.

2   Cut each slice into triangles, drizzle olive oil over them, and season with salt and pepper. Place them on a baking sheet, place it in the oven, and toast until they are crispy, about 6 minutes. Remove and let cool slightly before serving.

PAIRS WELL WITH: PICKLED VEGETABLES, FRUIT, FOIE GRAS

THYME & ASIAGO
Crackers

YIELD: 15 CRACKERS / **ACTIVE TIME:** 10 MINUTES / **TOTAL TIME:** 1 HOUR

INGREDIENTS

8 tablespoons unsalted butter

1 cup freshly grated Asiago cheese

Zest of 1 lemon

2 tablespoons chopped fresh thyme

1¼ cups all-purpose flour, plus more as needed

½ teaspoon kosher salt

¼ teaspoon black pepper

1 Place all the ingredients in a food processor and pulse until the mixture comes together as a dough.

2 Place the dough on a flour-dusted work surface and roll it into a 2-inch log. Cover tightly with plastic wrap and chill in the refrigerator for 30 minutes.

3 Preheat the oven to 350°F and line two baking sheets with parchment paper. Remove the dough from the refrigerator, cut it into ½-inch-thick slices, and place them on the baking sheets.

4 Place the crackers in the oven and bake until the crackers are golden brown, about 12 minutes. Remove from the oven and let the crackers cool before serving.

PAIRS WELL WITH: CREAMY SPREADS & CHEESES, HONEYCOMB, CURED MEATS

THYME & ASIAGO CRACKERS
SEE PAGE 53

YOGURT & BUCKWHEAT
Crackers

YIELD: 30 CRACKERS / ACTIVE TIME: 15 MINUTES / TOTAL TIME: 1 HOUR AND 30 MINUTES

INGREDIENTS

1½ cups buckwheat flour

1 teaspoon kosher salt

½ cup plain yogurt

8 tablespoons unsalted butter, softened, plus more as needed

Flaky sea salt, to taste

1   Place the flour, kosher salt, yogurt, and butter in a mixing bowl and work the mixture until it comes together as a dough.

2   Place the dough between two sheets of parchment paper and roll it out to about ¼ inch thick. Chill the dough in the refrigerator for 30 minutes.

3   Preheat the oven to 450°F and line two baking sheets with parchment paper. Place some butter in a skillet, melt it over medium heat, and set it aside.

4   Cut the dough into the desired shapes and place the crackers on the baking sheets. Brush each cracker with some of the melted butter and sprinkle the flaky sea salt over them.

5   Place them in the oven and bake until crisp, about 12 minutes. Remove from the oven and let the crackers cool completely before serving.

PAIRS WELL WITH: STONE FRUIT, BLUE CHEESES, SMOKED MEATS

CANDIED RITZ
Crackers

YIELD: 4 SERVINGS / **ACTIVE TIME:** 10 MINUTES / **TOTAL TIME:** 40 MINUTES

INGREDIENTS

10 tablespoons unsalted butter

1½ tablespoons brown sugar

6 oz. Ritz crackers

2 teaspoons kosher salt

1 teaspoon garlic powder

1 teaspoon onion powder

¼ teaspoon black pepper

¼ teaspoon red pepper flakes

1 teaspoon Old Bay seasoning

1 Preheat the oven to 350°F and line two baking sheets with parchment paper. Place the butter and brown sugar in a saucepan and melt over medium heat, stirring to combine.

2 Place the crackers in a large mixing bowl, pour the butter mixture over them, and gently stir to combine, taking care not to break the crackers.

3 Place the crackers on the baking sheets and sprinkle a bit of the remaining ingredients over each one. Place the sheets in the oven and bake until the glaze has hardened, about 12 minutes. Remove and let cool completely before serving.

PAIRS WELL WITH: SEAFOOD, PICKLED VEGETABLES, SUMMER-THEMED BOARDS

CHIA SEED
Crackers

YIELD: 30 CRACKERS / ACTIVE TIME: 20 MINUTES / TOTAL TIME: 2 HOURS

INGREDIENTS

9 tablespoons chia seeds

5 tablespoons water

½ cup almond flour

½ teaspoon kosher salt

¼ teaspoon black pepper

1 Use a spice grinder or a mortar and pestle to grind 1 tablespoon of the chia seeds into a powder. Transfer the powder to a bowl and add 3 tablespoons of the water. Gently stir to combine and let the mixture rest for 10 minutes.

2 Add the remaining chia seeds and water along with the almond flour, salt, and pepper. Fold until the mixture comes together as a dough, place it between two sheets of parchment paper, and roll out until it is approximately ¼ inch thick. Chill the dough in the refrigerator for 30 minutes.

3 Preheat the oven to 350°F and line two baking sheets with parchment paper. Cut the dough into the desired shapes and place them on the baking sheets.

4 Place them in the oven and bake until the crackers are golden brown, about 20 minutes. Remove from the oven and let the crackers cool completely before serving.

PAIRS WELL WITH: VEGAN & GLUTEN-FREE BOARDS, PICKLED VEGETABLES, NUTS

PECAN & BLUE CHEESE
Crackers

YIELD: 30 CRACKERS / ACTIVE TIME: 20 MINUTES / TOTAL TIME: 24 HOURS

INGREDIENTS

¾ cup pecans

¾ cup all-purpose flour

4 tablespoons unsalted butter, grated

3 oz. blue cheese

1 tablespoon fresh thyme, chopped

1 teaspoon kosher salt

1   Place all the ingredients in a food processor and pulse until the mixture comes together as a dough.

2   Place the dough between two sheets of parchment paper and roll it out until it is about ¼ inch thick. Place the dough in the refrigerator and chill for 24 hours.

3   Preheat the oven to 350°F and line two baking sheets with parchment paper. Cut the dough into the desired shapes, place them on the baking sheets, and bake in the oven until crispy, about 15 minutes. Remove from the oven and let cool before serving.

PAIRS WELL WITH: DUXELLES (SEE PAGE 349), BLUE CHEESES, COLD ROAST BEEF

LAVASH

YIELD: 4 LAVASH / **ACTIVE TIME:** 30 MINUTES / **TOTAL TIME:** 1 HOUR AND 30 MINUTES

INGREDIENTS

18 oz. all-purpose flour, plus more
as needed

14 oz. tepid water, plus more
as needed

1 teaspoon kosher salt

Extra-virgin olive oil, as needed

1   Combine the flour, water, and salt in the work bowl of a stand mixer fitted with the dough hook. Knead the mixture on low until it comes together as a smooth dough, about 5 minutes. If the dough is too dry, add a small amount of water. If the dough is too sticky, add a little bit of flour.

2   Place the dough on a flour-dusted work surface and knead it for 1 minute. Coat a mixing bowl with nonstick cooking spray, place the dough in the bowl, and cover it with plastic wrap. Let the dough sit at room temperature for 1 hour.

3   Preheat the oven to 500°F and place a baking stone on a rack in the middle of the oven.

4   Remove the dough from the bowl and place it on a flour-dusted work surface. Divide the dough into four equal pieces and roll them out until they are ¼-inch-thick ovals.

5   Working with one lavash at a time, use a pizza peel to carefully transfer the dough to the baking stone. Bake until the lavash begins to puff up and brown, 4 to 5 minutes.

6   Remove from the oven and immediately brush the lavash with olive oil. Place the cooked lavash in a basket, cover, and continue cooking the remaining lavash. Serve warm.

PAIRS WELL WITH: CREAMY SPREADS, MEDITERRANEAN-THEMED BOARDS,
HERB- & VEGETABLE-BASED CONDIMENTS

CHOCOLATE CHERRY
Crackers

YIELD: 30 CRACKERS / ACTIVE TIME: 15 MINUTES / TOTAL TIME: 1 HOUR AND 30 MINUTES

INGREDIENTS

½ cup all-purpose flour

½ cup wheat flour

¼ cup brown sugar

¼ cup cocoa powder

½ teaspoon fine sea salt

8 tablespoons unsalted butter, cold and cubed

3 tablespoons whole milk

½ cup dried cherries

⅓ cup sunflower seeds

1 Place all the ingredients in a food processor and pulse until the mixture comes together as a dough.

2 Place the dough between two sheets of parchment paper and roll out until it is ¼ inch thick. Place the dough in the refrigerator and chill for 45 minutes.

3 Preheat the oven to 350°F and line two baking sheets with parchment paper. Cut the dough into the desired shapes, place them on the baking sheets, and bake in the oven until crispy, about 12 minutes. Remove and let cool completely before serving.

PAIRS WELL WITH: GAME MEATS, HONEYCOMB, CREAMY CHEESES

RUM & CARAMELIZED
Banana Bread

YIELD: 1 LOAF / **ACTIVE TIME:** 30 MINUTES / **TOTAL TIME:** 2 HOURS

INGREDIENTS

2 cups all-purpose flour

1 teaspoon baking soda

¼ teaspoon cinnamon

¼ teaspoon allspice

½ teaspoon kosher salt

4 tablespoons unsalted butter, softened

3½ ripe bananas, sliced

4 oz. light brown sugar

2 tablespoons spiced rum

6 oz. sugar

½ cup extra-virgin olive oil

2 eggs

1½ teaspoons pure vanilla extract

2 tablespoons crème fraîche

1 Preheat the oven to 350°F. Coat an 8 x 4–inch loaf pan with nonstick cooking spray.

2 Place the flour, baking soda, cinnamon, allspice, and salt in a mixing bowl and whisk to combine. Set aside.

3 Place the butter in a large skillet and melt it over medium heat. Add the bananas and brown sugar and cook, stirring occasionally, until the bananas start to brown, about 3 minutes. Remove the pan from heat, stir in the rum, and let the mixture steep for 30 minutes.

4 In the work bowl of a stand mixer fitted with the paddle attachment, cream the caramelized banana mixture, sugar, olive oil, eggs, and vanilla on medium for 5 minutes. Add the dry mixture, reduce the speed to low, and beat until the mixture comes together as a smooth batter. Add the crème fraîche and beat to incorporate.

5 Pour the batter into the prepared loaf pan, place it in the oven, and bake until a cake tester inserted into the center of the banana bread loaf comes out clean, 60 to 70 minutes.

6 Remove the pan from the oven and place it on a wire rack to cool completely.

PAIRS WELL WITH: CREAMY & MILD CHEESES, BRUNCH BOARDS

ENGLISH
Muffins

YIELD: 8 MUFFINS / **ACTIVE TIME:** 30 MINUTES / **TOTAL TIME:** 3 HOURS

INGREDIENTS

7 oz. water

1 teaspoon active dry yeast

4½ teaspoons unsalted butter, softened

1 tablespoon sugar

1 egg

10 oz. bread flour, plus more as needed

1 teaspoon kosher salt

Semolina flour, as needed

1   Place the water and yeast in the work bowl of a stand mixer fitted with the dough hook, gently stir to combine, and let the mixture sit until it starts to foam, about 10 minutes.

2   Add the butter, sugar, egg, bread flour, and salt and knead on low for 1 minute. Raise the speed to medium and knead the mixture until it comes together as a smooth dough and begins to pull away from the side of the work bowl, about 5 minutes.

3   Coat a mixing bowl with nonstick cooking spray. Remove the dough from the work bowl, place it on a flour-dusted work surface, and shape it into a ball. Place the dough in the bowl, cover it with plastic wrap, place it in a naturally warm spot, and let it rise until doubled in size.

4   Line an 18 x 13–inch sheet pan with parchment paper.

5   Place the dough on a flour-dusted work surface and divide it into 2½-oz. portions. Flatten each ball into 3½-inch circle and place them on the pan. Cover with plastic wrap, place the muffins in a naturally warm spot, and let them rest for 30 minutes.

6   Warm a stovetop griddle over low heat and lightly sprinkle semolina on the griddle. Place the muffins on the griddle and cook until golden brown on both sides, 12 to 20 minutes. The internal temperature of the muffins should be 190°F. If the muffins browned too quickly and are not cooked through in the center, bake them in a 350°F oven for 5 to 10 minutes.

7   Let the muffins cool before slicing and enjoying.

ENGLISH MUFFINS
SEE PAGE 67

HONEY *Cornbread*

YIELD: 12 SERVINGS / ACTIVE TIME: 20 MINUTES / TOTAL TIME: 1 HOUR

INGREDIENTS

½ cup honey

12 oz. unsalted butter, softened

1 lb. all-purpose flour

8 oz. cornmeal

1 tablespoon baking powder, plus 1 teaspoon

1 tablespoon kosher salt

7 oz. sugar

4 eggs

2 cups milk

1   Preheat the oven to 350°F. Coat a 13 x 9–inch baking pan with nonstick cooking spray.

2   Place the honey and 4 oz. of the butter in a small saucepan and warm over medium heat until the butter has melted. Whisk to combine and set the mixture aside.

3   Place the flour, cornmeal, baking powder, and salt in a mixing bowl and whisk to combine. Set the mixture aside.

4   In the work bowl of a stand mixer fitted with the paddle attachment, cream the remaining butter and the sugar on medium until light and fluffy, about 5 minutes. Add the eggs and beat until incorporated. Add the dry mixture, reduce the speed to low, and beat until the mixture comes together as a smooth batter. Gradually add the milk and beat until incorporated.

5   Pour the batter into the pan, place the pan in the oven, and bake until a cake tester inserted into the center of the cornbread comes out clean, 25 to 30 minutes.

6   Remove from the oven and place the pan on a wire rack. Brush the cornbread with the honey butter and enjoy it warm.

PAIRS WELL WITH: SPICY FOODS, SWEET CONDIMENTS, GOAT CHEESE

SALTINES

YIELD: 30 CRACKERS / ACTIVE TIME: 30 MINUTES / TOTAL TIME: 2 HOURS

INGREDIENTS

12½ oz. water, at room temperature

1 tablespoon active dry yeast

½ cup extra-virgin olive oil

2 lbs. bread flour, plus more as needed

1 tablespoon kosher salt

Maldon sea salt, for topping

1   Place the water and yeast in the work bowl of a stand mixer, gently stir, and let the mixture sit until it starts to foam, about 10 minutes.

2   Add the olive oil to the work bowl and beat the mixture on medium for 1 minute. Add the flour and salt and beat the mixture until it comes together as a soft dough. Cover the dough in plastic wrap and chill it in the refrigerator for at least 1 hour.

3   Preheat the oven to 350°F. Line a 26 x 18–inch sheet pan with parchment paper.

4   Place the dough on a flour-dusted work surface and roll it out to ⅛ inch thick. Cut the dough into 2-inch squares, transfer them to the baking sheet, and use a fork to poke holes in each one. Sprinkle the sea salt over the crackers.

5   Place the crackers in the oven and bake them until the edges are golden brown, 12 to 15 minutes.

6   Remove the crackers from the oven, place the pan on a wire rack, and let them cool completely.

PAIRS WELL WITH: SEAFOOD, PICKLED VEGETABLES

STOUT
Gingerbread

YIELD: 1 LOAF / **ACTIVE TIME:** 15 MINUTES / **TOTAL TIME:** 1 HOUR AND 30 MINUTES

INGREDIENTS

10 oz. all-purpose flour

1½ teaspoons baking powder

2 tablespoons ground ginger

½ teaspoon cinnamon

½ teaspoon ground cloves

¼ teaspoon freshly grated nutmeg

¼ teaspoon kosher salt

1 cup molasses

1 cup stout

1½ teaspoons baking soda

3 eggs

4 oz. sugar

4 oz. dark brown sugar

¾ cup canola oil

1   Preheat the oven to 350°F. Coat an 8 x 4–inch loaf pan with nonstick cooking spray.

2   Place the flour, baking powder, ginger, cinnamon, cloves, nutmeg, and salt in a mixing bowl and whisk to combine. Set it aside.

3   Combine the molasses and stout in a small saucepan and bring it to a simmer over medium heat. Remove the pan from heat and whisk in the baking soda. Set the mixture aside.

4   In the work bowl of a stand mixer fitted with the paddle attachment, beat the eggs, sugar, brown sugar, and canola oil on medium until light and fluffy, about 5 minutes. Add the molasses mixture, beat until incorporated, and then add the dry mixture. Reduce the speed to low and beat until the mixture comes together as a smooth batter.

5   Pour the batter into the prepared loaf pan, place it in the oven, and bake until a cake tester inserted into the center of the loaf comes out clean, 50 to 60 minutes.

6   Remove the pan from the oven and place it on a wire rack to cool completely.

PAIRS WELL WITH: HOLIDAY-THEMED & DESSERT BOARDS, GAME MEATS, TART CONDIMENTS

BAGEL
Chips

YIELD: 4 SERVINGS / **ACTIVE TIME:** 10 MINUTES / **TOTAL TIME:** 25 MINUTES

INGREDIENTS

3 Everything Bagels (see page 90), sliced thin

1 Preheat the oven to 350°F.

2 Place the bagel slices on baking sheets and toast them in the oven until they are crispy and golden brown, about 8 minutes. Remove from the oven and let the chips cool slightly before enjoying.

PAIRS WELL WITH: BREAKFAST & BRUNCH BOARDS, SEAFOOD, CREAMY CHEESES & SPREADS

SOFT
Pretzels

YIELD: 4 SERVINGS / ACTIVE TIME: 45 MINUTES / TOTAL TIME: 2 HOURS

INGREDIENTS

½ cup warm water (105°F)

2 tablespoons brown sugar

¼ teaspoon instant yeast

6 tablespoons unsalted butter, melted

2½ teaspoons fine sea salt

4½ cups all-purpose flour

⅓ cup baking soda

1 egg

1 tablespoon water, at room temperature

Coarse sea salt, to taste

1   In the work bowl of a stand mixer fitted with the dough hook, combine the warm water, brown sugar, yeast, and melted butter and knead on low for 5 minutes.

2   Add the fine sea salt and flour, raise the speed to medium, and knead for another 4 minutes. Coat a large mixing bowl with nonstick cooking spray, transfer the dough to the bowl, and cover it with plastic wrap. Let the dough rest at room temperature until it has doubled in size, about 1 hour.

3   Cut the dough into ½-inch-thick ropes. Cut the ropes into bite-size pieces or twist them into traditional pretzel shapes.

4   Preheat the oven to 425°F. Line two baking sheets with parchment paper and coat with nonstick cooking spray. Bring water to a boil in a medium saucepan. Gradually add the baking soda and gently stir to combine.

5   Place the pretzels in the water and poach them briefly—30 seconds for bites, 1 minute for traditional pretzels. Carefully remove the pretzels with a slotted spoon and transfer them to the baking sheets.

6   Place the egg and room-temperature water in a small bowl, beat to combine, and brush the egg wash over the pretzels. Sprinkle the coarse sea salt over the pretzels and bake them in the oven until golden brown, about 15 minutes. Remove from the oven and briefly let cool before serving.

PAIRS WELL WITH: MILD CHEESES, GRAINY MUSTARD, PICKLED VEGETABLES

NORI
Crackers

YIELD: 30 CRACKERS / **ACTIVE TIME:** 30 MINUTES / **TOTAL TIME:** 45 MINUTES

INGREDIENTS

1 egg

1 tablespoon water

3 spring roll wrappers

3 sheets of nori

6 tablespoons sesame seeds

4 cups canola oil

Salt, to taste

1   Combine the egg and water and brush the spring roll wrappers with the egg wash. Place a sheet of nori on top of each wrapper and brush the nori with the egg wash. Sprinkle the sesame seeds on top and let them sit for 10 minutes.

2   Place the oil in a Dutch oven and warm it to 300°F over medium heat. Cut each sheet into nine squares, place them in the oil, and fry until browned and crispy, about 5 minutes. Transfer to a paper towel–lined plate, season with salt, and enjoy.

PAIRS WELL WITH: SEAFOOD, SPICY FOODS, PICKLED VEGETABLES

PARATHA

YIELD: 8 SERVINGS / **ACTIVE TIME:** 30 MINUTES / **TOTAL TIME:** 1 HOUR

INGREDIENTS

2 cups pastry flour, plus more as needed

1 cup whole wheat flour

¼ teaspoon kosher salt

1 cup warm water (105°F)

5 tablespoons extra-virgin olive oil, plus more as needed

5 tablespoons ghee or melted unsalted butter

1 Place the flours and salt in the work bowl of a stand mixer fitted with the paddle attachment. With the mixer running on low, slowly add the warm water. Mix until incorporated and then slowly add the olive oil. When the oil has been incorporated, place the dough on a lightly floured work surface and knead until it is quite smooth, about 8 minutes.

2 Divide the dough into 8 small balls and dust them with flour. Use your hands to roll each ball into a long rope, and then coil each rope into a large disk. Use a rolling pin to flatten the disks until they are no more than ¼ inch thick. Lightly brush each disk with a small amount of olive oil.

3 Place a cast-iron skillet over very high heat for about 4 minutes. Brush the surface with some of the ghee or melted butter and place a disk of the dough on the surface. Cook until it is blistered and brown, about 1 minute. Turn the paratha over and cook the other side. Transfer the cooked paratha to a plate and repeat with the remaining pieces of dough. Serve warm or at room temperature.

PAIRS WELL WITH: INDIAN-THEMED BOARDS, HERB-BASED CONDIMENTS, SPICY FOODS

CHEESE
Twists

YIELD: 12 SERVINGS / ACTIVE TIME: 15 MINUTES / TOTAL TIME: 30 MINUTES

INGREDIENTS

2 sheets of frozen puff pastry, thawed

All-purpose flour, as needed

½ cup grated Fontina cheese

½ cup grated Parmesan cheese

1 teaspoon finely chopped fresh thyme

1 teaspoon black pepper

1 egg, beaten

1   Preheat the oven to 375°F and line a baking sheet with parchment paper. Place the sheets of puff pastry on a flour-dusted surface and roll them out until the sheets are approximately 10 x 12–inch rectangles.

2   Place the cheeses, thyme, and pepper in a mixing bowl and stir to combine.

3   Lightly brush the tops of the pastry sheets with the egg. Sprinkle the cheese mixture over them and gently press down so it adheres to the pastry. Cut the sheets into ¼-inch-wide strips and twist them.

4   Place the twists on the baking sheet, place in the oven, and bake for 12 to 15 minutes, until the twists are golden brown and puffy. Turn the twists over and bake for another 2 to 3 minutes. Remove from the oven and let the twists cool on a wire rack before serving.

PAIR WELL WITH: NUTS, CURED MEATS

PITA
Bread

YIELD: 8 SERVINGS / ACTIVE TIME: 1 HOUR / TOTAL TIME: 3 HOURS

INGREDIENTS

1 cup lukewarm water (90°F)

1 tablespoon active dry yeast

1 tablespoon sugar

1¾ cups all-purpose flour, plus more as needed

1 cup whole wheat flour

1 tablespoon kosher salt

1   In a large mixing bowl, combine the water, yeast, and sugar. Let the mixture sit until it starts to foam, about 15 minutes.

2   Add the flours and salt and work the mixture until it comes together as a smooth dough. Cover the bowl with a linen towel and let it rise for about 15 minutes.

3   Preheat the oven to 500°F and place a baking stone on the floor of the oven.

4   Divide the dough into eight pieces and form them into balls. Place the balls on a flour-dusted work surface, press them down, and roll them until they are about ¼ inch thick.

5   Working with one pita at a time, place the pita on the baking stone and bake until it is puffy and brown, about 8 minutes. Remove from the oven and serve warm or at room temperature.

PAIRS WELL WITH: MEDITERRANEAN-THEMED BOARDS, CREAMY SPREADS & DIPS, SPICY FOODS

LAFFA

YIELD: 8 LAFFA / ACTIVE TIME: 30 MINUTES / TOTAL TIME: 1 HOUR AND 30 MINUTES

INGREDIENTS

1½ cups warm water (about 95°F), plus more as needed

2½ teaspoons active dry yeast

2 teaspoons sugar

2 cups all-purpose flour, plus more as needed

2 cups bread flour

1 teaspoon fine sea salt

2 tablespoons extra-virgin olive oil

1 In a mixing bowl, combine the water, yeast, and sugar, gently stir, and let stand until it starts to foam, 5 to 10 minutes.

2 Combine the flours and salt in the work bowl of a stand mixer fitted with the dough hook. Work the mixture on low until thoroughly combined.

3 Add the yeast mixture, another ½ cup water, and the olive oil to the work bowl and work the mixture on low until it comes together as a ball of dough and pulls away from the side of the work bowl.

4 Add another ½ cup water and continue to mix until it has been incorporated. The dough should feel tacky when slapped with a clean hand, but it should not be sticky. If it is too sticky, incorporate more flour, a tablespoon at a time.

5 Cover the dough with plastic wrap and let it rise at room temperature until doubled in size, about 1 hour.

6 Place a baking stone on a rack in the upper third of the oven and preheat it to 500°F.

7 Form the dough into 8 baseball-sized rounds and place them on a parchment-lined baking sheet. Cover with a linen towel and let the rounds rise until they are the size of softballs.

8 Place the balls on a flour-dusted work surface and roll them as thin as possible.

9 When the dough is rolled out and the baking stone is hot, carefully drape one laffa over your hand and then quickly lay the stretched laffa onto the baking stone, quickly pulling any wrinkles flat. Repeat with the remaining laffa.

10 Bake the laffa until puffy and cooked through, about 1 minute. Remove from the oven and enjoy immediately.

PAIRS WELL WITH: ROASTED VEGETABLES, MEATBALLS, MEDITERRANEAN-THEMED BOARDS

SOURDOUGH
Crackers

YIELD: 40 TO 80 CRACKERS / **ACTIVE TIME:** 30 MINUTES / **TOTAL TIME:** 2 HOURS

INGREDIENTS

1 cup Sourdough Starter
(see page 16)

1 cup all-purpose flour, plus
more as needed

½ teaspoon fine sea salt

4 tablespoons unsalted butter,
softened

Extra-virgin olive oil, as needed

Flaky sea salt (Maldon
recommended), to taste

1 Place the starter, flour, salt, and butter in a mixing bowl and work the mixture until it comes together as a smooth dough.

2 Divide the dough in half and form each piece into a rectangle. Cover the dough in plastic wrap and chill in the refrigerator until it is firm, about 1 hour.

3 Preheat the oven to 350°F. Dust a piece of parchment paper and a rolling pin with flour. Place one piece of dough on the parchment and roll it until it is about ¹⁄₁₆ inch thick.

4 Transfer the parchment, with the dough on it, to a baking sheet. Brush the dough with some olive oil and sprinkle the flaky sea salt over the top.

5 Cut the crackers to the desired size and shape and prick each cracker with a fork. Repeat with the remaining piece of dough.

6 Place the crackers in the oven and bake until crispy and golden brown, 20 to 25 minutes, rotating the baking sheets halfway through.

7 Remove the crackers from the oven, place the baking sheets on wire racks, and let the crackers cool completely before enjoying.

Note: Incorporate 2 to 3 tablespoons of herbs or seeds into the dough, and don't be afraid to experiment.

PAIRS WELL WITH: MILD CHEESES, CURED MEATS, HERB-BASED CONDIMENTS

EVERYTHING
Bagels

YIELD: 6 BAGELS / **ACTIVE TIME:** 1 HOUR / **TOTAL TIME:** 6 HOURS

INGREDIENTS

For the Dough

6 oz. water

¼ cup honey

1 egg white

1 tablespoon canola oil

2 teaspoons active dry yeast

1½ oz. sugar

19 oz. bread flour, plus more as needed

1½ teaspoons kosher salt

1 egg, beaten

For the Bath

12 cups water

½ cup honey

For the Everything Seasoning

2 tablespoons poppy seeds

1 tablespoon fennel seeds

1 tablespoon onion flakes

1 tablespoon garlic flakes

2 tablespoons sesame seeds

1 To begin preparations for the dough, place the water, honey, egg white, and canola oil in the work bowl of a stand mixer fitted with the dough hook and whisk to combine. Add the yeast, sugar, flour, and salt and work the mixture for 1 minute on low. Raise the speed to medium and knead the mixture until it comes together as a smooth dough and pulls away from the side of the work bowl, about 10 minutes.

2 Place the dough on a flour-dusted work surface and shape it into a ball. Return the dough to the work bowl, cover it with plastic wrap, and let the dough rise at room temperature until it has doubled in size.

3 Divide the dough into six 5-oz. pieces and form each one into a ball.

4 Coat an 18 x 13–inch sheet pan with nonstick cooking spray. Place the pieces of dough on the pan, cover them with plastic wrap, and let them rise until they have doubled in size.

5 Using your fingers to make a small hole in the centers of the balls of dough. Place both of your index fingers in the holes and, working in a rotating motion, slowly stretch the pieces of dough into 4-inch-wide bagels. Place the bagels on the sheet pan, cover them with plastic wrap, and let them sit for 30 minutes.

6 Preheat the oven to 350°F. To prepare the bath, place the ingredients in a wide saucepan and bring to a boil.

7 Gently place the bagels in the boiling water and poach them on each side for 30 seconds.

8 Place the bagels back on the sheet pan.

9 To prepare the everything seasoning, place all the ingredients in a mixing bowl and stir to combine.

10 Brush the bagels with the egg and sprinkle the seasoning mixture over them.

11 Place the bagels in the oven and bake until they are a deep golden brown, 20 to 25 minutes.

12 Remove the pan from the oven, place the bagels on a cooling rack, and let them cool before enjoying.

PAIRS WELL WITH: BREAKFAST & BRUNCH BOARDS, SMOKED SEAFOOD, CREAMY SPREADS

DIPS, SPREADS & CONDIMENTS

A good meal can be as easy as picking a few ripe tomatoes from the vine and whipping up some salsa, or covering a few toasted pieces of bread with a schmear of something decadent. The preparations in this chapter bring this pleasing simplicity within reach, and provide the bold with myriad opportunities to transform dishes in the other chapters.

APRICOT & CHILI
Jam

YIELD: 8 CUPS / **ACTIVE TIME:** 20 MINUTES / **TOTAL TIME:** 1 HOUR AND 30 MINUTES

INGREDIENTS

2 lbs. apricots, halved, pitted, and chopped

Zest and juice of 1 lemon

2 lbs. sugar

1 cup water

3 red chile peppers, seeded and minced

1 tablespoon unsalted butter

1 Place all the ingredients, except for the butter, in a saucepan and bring to a gentle boil over medium heat, stirring to help the sugar dissolve. Boil the mixture for about 5 minutes.

2 Reduce the heat and simmer for 15 minutes, stirring frequently. If you prefer a smoother jam, mash the mixture with a wooden spoon as it cooks.

3 When the jam has formed a thin skin, remove the pan from the heat. Add the butter and stir to disperse any froth. Remove and let cool for 15 minutes. To can this jam, see page 325. If you are not interested in canning it, let the jam cool completely before storing in the refrigerator.

PAIRS WELL WITH: SUMMER-THEMED & BRUNCH BOARDS, CURED MEATS

PEA & PARMESAN
Dip

YIELD: 2 CUPS / **ACTIVE TIME:** 10 MINUTES / **TOTAL TIME:** 20 MINUTES

INGREDIENTS

Salt and pepper, to taste

3 cups peas

1 cup water

3 tablespoons pine nuts

1 cup freshly grated Parmesan cheese

1 garlic clove, minced

½ cup fresh mint, chiffonade

1   Bring water to a boil in a large saucepan. Add salt and the peas and cook until the peas are bright green and warmed through, about 2 minutes.

2   Transfer half of the peas to a food processor. Add the water, pine nuts, Parmesan, and garlic and blitz until pureed.

3   Place the puree in a serving dish, add the remaining peas and the mint, and fold to incorporate. Season the dip with salt and pepper and chill in the refrigerator until ready to serve.

PAIRS WELL WITH: CROSTINI (SEE PAGE 51), CRUDITÉS, CHEESY CRACKERS

GREEN TOMATO
Jam

YIELD: 2 CUPS / **ACTIVE TIME:** 35 MINUTES / **TOTAL TIME:** 5 TO 7 HOURS

INGREDIENTS

12 oz. green tomatoes, diced

¼ large onion, diced

½-inch piece of fresh ginger, peeled and minced

2 garlic cloves, chopped

1 teaspoon mustard seeds

1 teaspoon cumin

1 teaspoon coriander

2 teaspoons kosher salt

½ cup honey or maple syrup

1 cup apple cider vinegar

1 cup raisins

1   Place all the ingredients in a large saucepan and bring to a boil. Reduce the heat so that the mixture simmers and cook, stirring occasionally, until the onions and tomatoes are tender and the juices have thickened, 20 to 30 minutes. If a smoother jam is desired, mash the mixture with a wooden spoon as it simmers.

2   Remove the pan from heat. To can this jam, see page 325. If you are not interested in canning it, let cool completely before storing in the refrigerator.

PAIRS WELL WITH: FRIED FOODS, SUMMER-THEMED BOARDS

WHIPPED HERB
Butter

YIELD: ½ CUP / **ACTIVE TIME:** 10 MINUTES / **TOTAL TIME:** 10 MINUTES

INGREDIENTS

8 tablespoons unsalted butter

1 tablespoon extra-virgin olive oil

1 garlic clove, minced

1 tablespoon fresh thyme

1 tablespoon chopped fresh basil

1   Place the butter in a mixing bowl and beat with a handheld mixer at medium speed until it is pale and fluffy.

2   Add the olive oil, garlic, and herbs to the butter and beat until incorporated.

3   Serve immediately or store the butter in the refrigerator until ready to serve.

PAIRS WELL WITH: CRUSTY BREADS, SPRING- & SUMMER-THEMED BOARDS, SOURDOUGH CRACKERS (SEE PAGE 89)

CREAMY QUARK &
Mozzarella Dip

YIELD: 6 SERVINGS / **ACTIVE TIME:** 20 MINUTES / **TOTAL TIME:** 1 HOUR AND 45 MINUTES

INGREDIENTS

1 cup quark cheese, softened

½ cup sour cream

1 cup shredded mozzarella cheese, plus more as needed

2 tablespoons chopped fresh rosemary

2 tablespoons fresh thyme

½ cup diced summer squash

1 cup chopped Swiss chard leaves

1 cup spinach

6 garlic cloves, diced

2 teaspoons kosher salt

1 teaspoon black pepper

1 Place the quark, sour cream, and mozzarella in an oven-safe bowl and stir until well combined.

2 Add the remaining ingredients, stir to combine, and place in the refrigerator for at least 1 hour.

3 Approximately 30 minutes before you are ready to serve the dip, preheat the oven to 350°F. Top the dip with additional mozzarella and bake until the cheese is melted and slightly brown, about 20 minutes. Remove from the oven and let cool briefly before serving.

PAIRS WELL WITH: CRUDITÉS, SPICY FOODS, CRUSTY BREADS

BLUEBERRY &
Basil Jam

YIELD: 3½ CUPS / **ACTIVE TIME:** 10 MINUTES / **TOTAL TIME:** 1 HOUR AND 30 MINUTES

INGREDIENTS

3 quarts of fresh blueberries

Leaves from 1 bunch of basil, finely chopped

2 teaspoons fresh lemon juice

2 cups sugar

½ cup water

1   Place all the ingredients in a large saucepan and bring to a boil, while stirring frequently, over medium-high heat.

2   Once the mixture has come to a boil, reduce the heat so that it simmers and cook, stirring frequently, until the mixture has reduced by half and is starting to thicken, about 1 hour. Remove from heat and let it thicken and set as it cools. If the jam is still too thin after 1 hour, continue to simmer until it is the desired consistency.

3   To can this jam, see page 325. If you are not interested in canning it, let cool completely before storing in the refrigerator.

PAIRS WELL WITH: SAVORY QUICKBREADS, SUMMER-THEMED BOARDS, CURED MEATS

CULTURED
Butter

YIELD: 2 CUPS / **ACTIVE TIME:** 10 MINUTES / **TOTAL TIME:** 2 DAYS

INGREDIENTS

4 cups high-quality heavy cream

½ cup whole milk yogurt

½ teaspoon kosher salt

1   Place the heavy cream and yogurt in a jar. Seal it and shake vigorously to combine.

2   Open the jar, cover it with cheesecloth, and secure it with a rubber band or kitchen twine.

3   Place the mixture away from direct sunlight and let it sit at room temperature for 36 hours.

4   After 36 hours, seal the jar and place it in the refrigerator for 4 to 6 hours.

5   Remove the mixture from the refrigerator and pour it into the work bowl of a stand mixer fitted with the whisk attachment. Add the salt and whip on high, covering with a towel to prevent spilling, until the butter separates from the buttermilk. Reserve the buttermilk for another preparation.

6   Transfer the butter to a piece of cheesecloth and squeeze out any excess liquid. Wash the butter under ice-cold water and store in an airtight container. It will keep in the refrigerator for approximately 3 months.

PAIRS WELL WITH: CRUSTY BREADS, GOAT CHEESE

PORK
Pâté

YIELD: 10 TO 12 SERVINGS / **ACTIVE TIME:** 20 MINUTES / **TOTAL TIME:** 24 HOURS

INGREDIENTS

3- to 5-lb. bone-in pork shoulder

3 onions, sliced

2 teaspoons ground cloves

1 tablespoon kosher salt, plus more to taste

4 bay leaves

2 teaspoons black pepper, plus more to taste

1 teaspoon freshly grated nutmeg

1. Preheat the oven to 300°F. Place all the ingredients in a Dutch oven and stir to combine. Cover, place in the oven, and braise until the pork falls apart at the touch of a fork, about 3 to 4 hours.

2. Remove from the oven, discard the bay leaves, and transfer the pork shoulder to a plate. When the pork shoulder has cooled slightly, shred it with a fork.

3. Place the shredded pork and ½ cup of the cooking liquid in a blender. Puree until it forms a paste, adding more cooking liquid as needed to achieve the desired consistency.

4. Season with salt and pepper, transfer the paste to a large jar, and then pour the remaining cooking liquid over it. Cover the jar and store it in the refrigerator overnight before serving.

PAIRS WELL WITH: PICKLED VEGETABLES, CREAMY CHEESES, AUTUMN-THEMED BOARDS

BAGNA
Cauda

YIELD: 4 SERVINGS / **ACTIVE TIME:** 20 MINUTES / **TOTAL TIME:** 30 MINUTES

INGREDIENTS

½ cup quality anchovy fillets, rinsed, boned, and chopped

⅔ cup extra-virgin olive oil

2 tablespoons unsalted butter

4 garlic cloves, mashed with a mortar and pestle

Salt, to taste

1   Place the anchovies in a mortar and use a pestle to grind them into a paste. Set the anchovies aside.

2   Place 2 tablespoons of the olive oil and all of the butter in a small saucepan and warm over low heat. When the butter has melted, add the garlic, reduce the heat to the lowest possible setting, and cook, stirring to ensure that the garlic does not brown, for 5 minutes.

3   Add the anchovies and cook for 5 minutes, stirring occasionally. Cook until the mixture starts to darken, stir in the rest of the olive oil along with a pinch of salt, and cook at below a simmer for 15 to 20 minutes. If the mixture starts to sizzle, turn off the heat for a minute or so.

4   Serve warm with sliced raw vegetables for dipping. If the bagna cauda cools down, return it to the stove and warm it up again.

PAIRS WELL WITH: CRUDITÉS, BREADS, ITALIAN-THEMED BOARDS

MOSTARDA

YIELD: 1 CUP / **ACTIVE TIME:** 5 MINUTES / **TOTAL TIME:** 15 MINUTES

INGREDIENTS

4 oz. dried apricots, chopped

¼ cup chopped dried cherries

1 shallot, minced

1½ teaspoons minced crystallized ginger

½ cup dry white wine

3 tablespoons white wine vinegar

3 tablespoons water

3 tablespoons sugar

1 teaspoon mustard powder

1 teaspoon Dijon mustard

1 tablespoon unsalted butter

1 Place the apricots, cherries, shallot, ginger, wine, vinegar, water, and sugar in a saucepan and bring to a boil over medium-high heat. Cover, reduce the heat to medium, and cook until all the liquid has been absorbed and the fruit is soft, about 10 minutes.

2 Uncover the pot and stir in the mustard powder, mustard, and butter. Simmer until the mixture is jam-like, 2 to 3 minutes. Remove from heat and let cool slightly before serving. The mostarda will keep in the refrigerator for up to 1 week.

PAIRS WELL WITH: CRUSTY BREADS, CURED MEATS, MILD CHEESES

CILANTRO
Pesto

YIELD: 1½ CUPS / **ACTIVE TIME:** 5 MINUTES / **TOTAL TIME:** 5 MINUTES

INGREDIENTS

1 cup fresh cilantro

1 garlic clove

¼ cup roasted and shelled
sunflower seeds

¼ cup shredded queso enchilado

¼ cup extra-virgin olive oil

1 teaspoon fresh lemon juice

Salt and pepper, to taste

1   Place of the ingredients in a food processor and blitz until emulsified and smooth. Chill in the refrigerator until ready to serve.

PAIRS WELL WITH: CRUSTY BREADS, SPICY FOODS

GUACAMOLE

YIELD: 4 SERVINGS / **ACTIVE TIME:** 15 MINUTES / **TOTAL TIME:** 25 MINUTES

INGREDIENTS

1 large tomato, finely diced

2 serrano chile peppers, finely diced

½ onion, finely diced

1 garlic clove, mashed

4 large avocados, pitted and diced

6 tablespoons fresh lime juice

Salt, to taste

½ cup fresh cilantro, chopped

1 Combine the tomato, serrano peppers, and onion in a bowl. Place the garlic clove in a separate bowl.

2 Add the avocados to the bowl containing the garlic and stir until well combined. Stir in the lime juice and season with salt.

3 Add the tomato mixture and stir until it has been incorporated. Add the cilantro and stir to combine. Taste and adjust the seasoning as necessary.

PAIRS WELL WITH: TORTILLA CHIPS, CRUDITÉS

SWEET CORN &
Pepita Guacamole

YIELD: 4 SERVINGS / **ACTIVE TIME:** 15 MINUTES / **TOTAL TIME:** 30 MINUTES

INGREDIENTS

1 ear of yellow corn, with husk on

1 oz. pumpkin seeds

1 oz. pomegranate seeds

Flesh of 3 avocados

½ red onion, chopped

½ cup fresh cilantro, chopped

1 teaspoon fresh lime juice

Salt and pepper, to taste

1 Preheat a gas or charcoal grill to medium-high heat (about 450°F). Place the corn on the grill and cook until it is charred all over and the kernels have softened enough that there is considerable give in them.

2 Remove the corn from the grill and let it cool. When cool enough to handle, husk the corn and cut off the kernels.

3 Combine the corn, pumpkin seeds, and pomegranate seeds in a small bowl. Place the avocados in a separate bowl and mash until it is just slightly chunky. Stir in the corn mixture, onion, cilantro, and lime juice, season the mixture with salt and pepper, and work the mixture until the guacamole is the desired texture.

PAIRS WELL WITH: TORTILLA CHIPS, CRUDITÉS, SPICY FOODS

SWEET CORN & PEPITA GUACAMOLE
SEE PAGE 115

SALSA

de Chiltomate

YIELD: 1½ CUPS / **ACTIVE TIME:** 20 MINUTES / **TOTAL TIME:** 1 HOUR

INGREDIENTS

8½ oz. Roma tomatoes, halved

2 habanero chile peppers

1 small white onion, quartered

4 garlic cloves, unpeeled

2 tablespoons extra-virgin olive oil

Salt, to taste

Juice of 1 lime

1   Preheat the oven to 450°F. Line a baking sheet with parchment paper, place the tomatoes, chiles, onion, and garlic on it, and place it in the oven.

2   Roast until the vegetables are charred all over, checking every 5 minutes or so and removing them as they become ready.

3   Peel the garlic cloves, remove the stem and seeds from the habanero (gloves are strongly recommended while handling habaneros), and place the roasted vegetables in a blender. Puree until smooth.

4   Place the olive oil in a medium saucepan and warm it over medium-high heat. Carefully pour the puree into the pan, reduce the heat, and simmer until it has reduced slightly and the flavor is to your liking, 15 to 20 minutes.

5   Season with salt, stir in the lime juice, and let the salsa cool. Taste, adjust the seasoning as necessary, and enjoy.

PAIRS WELL WITH: TORTILLA CHIPS, MILD CHEESES

SALSA
Verde

YIELD: 1½ CUPS / **ACTIVE TIME:** 20 MINUTES / **TOTAL TIME:** 30 MINUTES

INGREDIENTS

1 lb. tomatillos, husked and rinsed

5 garlic cloves, unpeeled

1 small white onion, quartered

10 serrano chile peppers

2 bunches of fresh cilantro

Salt, to taste

1 Warm a cast-iron skillet over high heat. Place the tomatillos, garlic, onion, and chiles in the pan and cook until charred all over, turning them occasionally.

2 Remove the vegetables from the pan and let them cool slightly.

3 Peel the garlic cloves and remove the stems and seeds from the chiles. Place the charred vegetables in a blender, add the cilantro, and puree until smooth.

4 Season the salsa with salt and enjoy.

PAIRS WELL WITH: TORTILLA CHIPS, CRUDITÉS, AUTUMN-THEMED BOARDS

SALSA
Borracha

YIELD: 1½ CUPS / **ACTIVE TIME:** 20 MINUTES / **TOTAL TIME:** 30 MINUTES

INGREDIENTS

8 oz. tomatillos, husked and rinsed

¾ small white onion

5 garlic cloves, unpeeled

2 tablespoons lard

3 pasilla chile peppers, stemmed and seeded

2 chipotle morita chile peppers, stemmed and seeded

3½ oz. Mexican lager

1 teaspoon mezcal or tequila

1 teaspoon Maggi seasoning sauce

Salt, to taste

1 Warm a cast-iron skillet over medium-high heat. Add the tomatillos, onion, and garlic and toast until charred all over, turning them as needed. Remove the vegetables from the pan and let them cool. When cool enough to handle, peel the garlic cloves and place the mixture in a blender.

2 Place half of the lard in the skillet and warm it over medium heat. Add the chiles and fry until fragrant and pliable. Place the chiles in the blender.

3 Add the beer, mezcal, and Maggi and puree until smooth.

4 Place the remaining lard in a saucepan and warm it over medium heat. Add the puree and fry it for 5 minutes. Season the salsa with salt and let it cool before enjoying.

PAIRS WELL WITH: DARK BEERS, SMOKED MEATS, SMOKED CHEESES, TORTILLA CHIPS

HABANERO
Honey

YIELD: 1 CUP / **ACTIVE TIME:** 10 MINUTES / **TOTAL TIME:** 2 HOURS

INGREDIENTS

4 habanero chile peppers, pierced

1 cup honey

1. Place the chili peppers and honey in a saucepan and bring to a very gentle simmer over medium-low heat. Reduce heat to lowest possible setting and cook for 1 hour.

2. Remove the saucepan from heat and let the mixture infuse for another hour.

3. Remove the peppers. Transfer the honey to a container, cover, and chill in the refrigerator until ready to serve.

PAIRS WELL WITH: SEAFOOD, POULTRY, NUTS

BALSAMIC
Ranch

YIELD: 2 CUPS / **ACTIVE TIME:** 5 MINUTES / **TOTAL TIME:** 5 MINUTES

INGREDIENTS

½ cup mayonnaise

½ cup sour cream

½ cup buttermilk

3 tablespoons balsamic vinegar

¼ teaspoon onion powder

½ teaspoon garlic powder

2 teaspoons chopped fresh parsley

1 Place all the ingredients in a mixing bowl and whisk until the mixture is thoroughly combined.

2 Taste, adjust the seasoning as necessary, and refrigerate until ready to serve.

PAIRS WELL WITH: STRONG-FLAVORED CHEESES, CRUDITÉS, CURED MEATS

ROASTED GARLIC
Aioli

YIELD: 2 SERVINGS / **ACTIVE TIME:** 10 MINUTES / **TOTAL TIME:** 40 MINUTES

INGREDIENTS

1 head of garlic

½ cup extra-virgin olive oil, plus more as needed

Salt and pepper, to taste

1 egg yolk

1 teaspoon fresh lemon juice

1 Preheat the oven to 350°F. Cut off the top ½ inch of the head of garlic. Place the remainder in a piece of aluminum foil, drizzle olive oil over it, and season it with salt.

2 Place the garlic in the oven and roast until the garlic cloves have softened and are caramelized, about 30 minutes. Remove from the oven, remove the cloves from the head of garlic, and place them in a mixing bowl.

3 Add the egg yolk and lemon juice and whisk to combine. While whisking continually, add the olive oil in a slow stream. When all the oil has been emulsified, season the aioli with salt and pepper and serve.

PAIRS WELL WITH: BEEF, BOLD CHEESES, CROSTINI (SEE PAGE 51)

TZATZIKI

YIELD: ½ CUP / **ACTIVE TIME:** 10 MINUTES / **TOTAL TIME:** 1 HOUR AND 10 MINUTES

INGREDIENTS

1 cucumber, sliced thin

1 garlic clove, minced

1 teaspoon kosher salt

½ cup Greek yogurt

1 tablespoon chopped fresh mint

1   Place the cucumber, garlic, and salt in a mixing bowl and let it rest for 1 hour.

2   Strain the cucumber mixture and reserve the liquid. Place the cucumber mixture in a mixing bowl, add the yogurt and mint, and stir to combine.

3   Incorporate the reserved liquid 1 teaspoon at a time until the tzatziki has the desired texture and then chill it in the refrigerator until ready to serve.

PAIRS WELL WITH: CRUDITÉS, FLATBREADS, SPICY FOODS

BACON

Jam

YIELD: ½ CUP / **ACTIVE TIME:** 20 MINUTES / **TOTAL TIME:** 1 HOUR

INGREDIENTS

8 oz. bacon

½ white onion, minced

1 garlic clove, minced

2 tablespoons apple cider vinegar

2 tablespoons brown sugar

1 tablespoon maple syrup

1. Preheat the oven to 350°F. Set a wire rack in a rimmed baking sheet, place the bacon on the rack, and place the sheet in the oven. Bake the bacon until it is crispy, about 10 minutes.

2. Remove the bacon from the oven and transfer it to a paper towel–lined plate to drain. Reserve the bacon fat. When the bacon is cool enough to handle, chop it into small pieces.

3. Place the reserved bacon fat in a large skillet and warm it over medium heat. Add the onion and cook, stirring frequently, until it has softened, about 5 minutes.

4. Stir in the bacon and the remaining ingredients, bring the mixture to a simmer, and cook until it has thickened slightly. Transfer the mixture to a bowl and let it chill in the refrigerator before serving.

PAIRS WELL WITH: BLUE CHEESES, STONE FRUIT, FIGS

ITALIAN DIPPING
Oil

YIELD: 1½ CUPS / **ACTIVE TIME:** 5 MINUTES / **TOTAL TIME:** 5 MINUTES

INGREDIENTS

1 tablespoon black pepper

2 tablespoons herbes de Provence

1 tablespoon dried thyme

1 tablespoon dried mint

1 tablespoon dried oregano

1 tablespoon garlic powder

3 garlic cloves, minced

1 teaspoon kosher salt

1 teaspoon red pepper flakes

1 cup extra-virgin olive oil

¼ cup balsamic vinegar

1   Combine all the ingredients, except for the balsamic vinegar, in a mixing bowl and let the mixture sit at room temperature until ready to serve.

2   Stir in the balsamic vinegar right before serving.

PAIRS WELL WITH: CRUSTY BREADS, MILD & CREAMY CHEESES

TEQUILA
Cheese Dip

YIELD: 4 SERVINGS / **ACTIVE TIME:** 10 MINUTES / **TOTAL TIME:** 25 MINUTES

INGREDIENTS

6 oz. Oaxaca cheese, cubed

½ plum tomato, diced

¼ white onion, diced

2 tablespoons diced green chile peppers

2 tablespoons sugar

¼ cup fresh lime juice

1 teaspoon chili powder

1 oz. tequila

1 Preheat the oven to 350°F. Place the cheese, tomato, onion, and chiles in a small cast-iron skillet and stir to combine. Set the mixture aside.

2 Combine the sugar, lime juice, and chili powder in a small saucepan and cook over medium heat, stirring to dissolve the sugar, until the mixture is syrupy.

3 Drizzle the syrup over the cheese mixture, place it in the oven, and bake until the cheese has melted and is golden brown on top, about 15 minutes.

4 Remove the pan from the oven, pour the tequila over the mixture, and use a long match or a wand lighter to ignite it. Bring the flaming skillet to the table and enjoy once the flames have gone out.

PAIRS WELL WITH: TORTILLA CHIPS, SPICY FOODS, CRUDITÉS

CRAB
Dip

YIELD: 4 SERVINGS / **ACTIVE TIME:** 15 MINUTES / **TOTAL TIME:** 50 MINUTES

INGREDIENTS

1 tablespoon unsalted butter

½ shallot, minced

¼ cup panko

Salt, to taste

1½ teaspoons dry vermouth

5 oz. cream cheese, softened

¼ cup crème fraîche

¼ cup mayonnaise

1 tablespoon Dijon mustard

¼ cup chopped fresh chives

8 oz. lump crabmeat

½ teaspoon cayenne pepper

½ teaspoon Old Bay seasoning

1   Preheat the oven to 350°F. Place the butter in a skillet and melt it over medium heat. Add the shallot and cook, stirring frequently, until it has softened, about 4 minutes.

2   Stir in the panko and cook until golden brown, 2 to 4 minutes. Remove the pan from heat.

3   Combine the panko mixture and the remaining ingredients in a mixing bowl and then transfer the mixture to a ramekin or a crock. Place the dip in the oven and bake until golden brown on top, about 35 minutes. Remove from the oven and serve immediately.

PAIRS WELL WITH: BUTTERY CRACKERS, SUMMER-THEMED BOARDS

SULTANA & MANGO
Chutney

YIELD: 1 CUP / **ACTIVE TIME:** 10 MINUTES / **TOTAL TIME:** 20 MINUTES

INGREDIENTS

1½ tablespoons extra-virgin olive oil

½ red onion, diced

½ teaspoon red pepper flakes

½ teaspoon curry powder

½ teaspoon grated fresh ginger

1 garlic clove, minced

⅓ cup red wine vinegar

½ cup mango jam

¼ cup sultanas (golden raisins)

⅓ cup water

1 Place the olive oil in a large skillet and warm it over medium heat. When the oil starts to shimmer, add the onion, red pepper flakes, and curry powder and cook, stirring frequently, until the onion starts to soften, about 3 minutes.

2 Stir in the ginger and garlic, cook for 1 minute, and then add the remaining ingredients. Bring to a simmer and cook until the mixture has reduced. Transfer to a serving dish and serve warm or at room temperature.

PAIRS WELL WITH: POULTRY, GOAT CHEESE, SPICY NUTS

POMEGRANATE
Reduction

YIELD: ½ CUP / **ACTIVE TIME:** 10 MINUTES / **TOTAL TIME:** 10 MINUTES

INGREDIENTS

8 oz. pomegranate juice

1 Place the juice in a saucepan and cook over medium heat until it is thick enough to coat the back of a wooden spoon. Remove from heat and let cool before serving.

PAIRS WELL WITH: MILD CHEESES, POULTRY, SPICY NUTS

RASPBERRY & CHIA
Jam

YIELD: 2 CUPS / **ACTIVE TIME:** 20 MINUTES / **TOTAL TIME:** 1 HOUR AND 30 MINUTES

INGREDIENTS

2 cups raspberries

2 tablespoons water

1 tablespoon fresh lemon juice

3 tablespoons chia seeds

3 tablespoons honey

1   Place the raspberries and water in a saucepan and cook the mixture over medium heat for 2 minutes.

2   Stir in the remaining ingredients and cook until the mixture has thickened and acquired a jammy consistency. Remove from heat and let the jam cool completely before serving.

PAIRS WELL WITH: WHOLE WHEAT CRACKERS, PICKLED VEGETABLES

CRANBERRY
Relish

YIELD: 2 CUPS / **ACTIVE TIME:** 5 MINUTES / **TOTAL TIME:** 1 HOUR

INGREDIENTS

12 oz. cranberries

1 Granny Smith apple, cored and diced

Segments of ½ orange

1 cup sugar

1 Place the cranberries in a food processor and pulse for 1 minute. Add the apple and orange and pulse until combined. Add the sugar and pulse until incorporated.

2 Transfer the mixture to a bowl and let it macerate for at least 1 hour before serving.

PAIRS WELL WITH: GAME MEATS, DARK BREADS, NUTTY CHEESES

ORANGE
Marmalade

YIELD: 2 CUPS / **ACTIVE TIME:** 30 MINUTES / **TOTAL TIME:** 4 HOURS

INGREDIENTS

2 oranges, sliced

2 lemons, sliced

4 cups water

4 cups sugar

1   Place the ingredients in a large saucepan fitted with a candy thermometer. Cook over medium-low heat, stirring occasionally, until the mixture reaches 220°F, about 2 hours.

2   Pour the marmalade into a mason jar and let it cool completely before serving.

PAIRS WELL WITH: BREAKFAST & BRUNCH BOARDS, CURED MEATS, SWEET & CREAMY CHEESES

BEER Cheese

YIELD: 4 SERVINGS / **ACTIVE TIME:** 20 MINUTES / **TOTAL TIME:** 20 MINUTES

INGREDIENTS

2 tablespoons unsalted butter

1½ teaspoons all-purpose flour

¾ cup brown ale

1 tablespoon Worcestershire sauce

½ teaspoon mustard powder

Pinch of cayenne pepper

1½ cups grated cheddar cheese

Salt and pepper, to taste

1 Place the butter in a saucepan and melt it over medium heat. Add the flour and cook, stirring constantly, until the mixture starts to brown, about 2 minutes.

2 Deglaze the pan with the brown ale and Worcestershire sauce, scraping up any browned bits from the bottom.

3 Add the remaining ingredients, cook until the cheese has melted, and serve immediately.

PAIRS WELL WITH: PRETZELS, SAUSAGES, CORNICHONS

MIGNONETTE
Sauce

YIELD: ½ CUP / **ACTIVE TIME:** 5 MINUTES / **TOTAL TIME:** 5 MINUTES

INGREDIENTS

½ cup red wine vinegar

1½ tablespoons minced shallot

½ teaspoon freshly cracked
black pepper

1   Place the ingredients in a bowl, stir to combine, and chill in the refrigerator
for 1 hour before serving.

PAIRS WELL WITH: OYSTERS, SUMMER-THEMED BOARDS

ROASTED ARTICHOKE &
Spinach Dip

YIELD: 1 CUP / **ACTIVE TIME:** 5 MINUTES / **TOTAL TIME:** 15 MINUTES

INGREDIENTS

¾ lb. artichoke hearts, quartered

4 garlic cloves, unpeeled

2 cups baby spinach

2 tablespoons apple cider vinegar

¼ teaspoon kosher salt

¼ cup extra-virgin olive oil

Pinch of onion powder (optional)

1   Preheat the oven's broiler to high. Place the artichoke hearts and garlic on a baking sheet and broil, turning them occasionally, until browned all over, about 10 minutes. Remove from the oven and let cool. When cool enough to handle, peel the garlic cloves.

2   Place the artichoke hearts and garlic in a food processor, add the remaining ingredients, and blitz until the spread has the desired texture.

PAIRS WELL WITH: CRUDITÉS, FLATBREADS, TORTILLA CHIPS

GREEN GODDESS
Dip

YIELD: 6 CUPS / **ACTIVE TIME:** 5 MINUTES / **TOTAL TIME:** 5 MINUTES

INGREDIENTS

1½ cups mayonnaise

2 cups sour cream

1 tablespoon chopped fresh parsley

1 tablespoon chopped fresh tarragon

1 tablespoon chopped fresh chives

1 tablespoon chopped fresh basil

1 tablespoon red wine vinegar

1 tablespoon sugar

1 teaspoon garlic powder

1 tablespoon Worcestershire sauce

Salt and pepper, to taste

6 oz. blue cheese

1 Place all the ingredients, except for the blue cheese, in a food processor and blitz until pureed.

2 Add the blue cheese and pulse a few times, making sure to maintain a chunky texture. Store the dip in the refrigerator until ready to serve.

PAIRS WELL WITH: CRUSTY BREADS, CURED MEATS

PESTO

YIELD: 2 CUPS / **ACTIVE TIME:** 10 MINUTES / **TOTAL TIME:** 10 MINUTES

INGREDIENTS

2 cups packed fresh basil leaves

1 cup packed fresh baby spinach

2 cups freshly grated Parmesan cheese

¼ cup pine nuts

1 garlic clove

2 teaspoons fresh lemon juice

Salt and pepper, to taste

½ cup extra-virgin olive oil

1   Place all the ingredients, except for the olive oil, in a food processor and pulse until pureed.

2   Transfer the puree to a mixing bowl. While whisking, add the olive oil in a slow stream until it is emulsified. Serve immediately or store in the refrigerator.

PAIRS WELL WITH: CROSTINI (SEE PAGE 51), SLICED TOMATOES, CURED MEATS

WHITE BEAN &
Rosemary Spread

YIELD: 2 CUPS / **ACTIVE TIME:** 5 MINUTES / **TOTAL TIME:** 35 MINUTES

INGREDIENTS

1 (14 oz.) can of cannellini beans, drained and rinsed

2 tablespoons extra-virgin olive oil

2 teaspoons balsamic vinegar

2 garlic cloves, minced

1 tablespoon chopped fresh rosemary

½ celery stalk, peeled and minced

Salt and pepper, to taste

2 pinches of red pepper flakes

1 Place half of the beans in a bowl and mash them until they are smooth.

2 Add the rest of the beans, the olive oil, vinegar, garlic, rosemary, and celery and stir to combine.

3 Season the dip with salt, pepper, and red pepper flakes and cover the bowl with plastic wrap. Let the dip sit so that the flavors combine for about 30 minutes before serving.

PAIRS WELL WITH: CRUDITÉS, MEATBALLS, FLATBREADS

ROASTED PUMPKIN
Dip

YIELD: 6 TO 8 SERVINGS / **ACTIVE TIME:** 5 MINUTES / **TOTAL TIME:** 35 MINUTES

INGREDIENTS

1 (3 lb.) sugar pumpkin, halved and seeded

5 tablespoons extra-virgin olive oil

2 teaspoons kosher salt

1 teaspoon black pepper

1 teaspoon fresh thyme

¼ teaspoon freshly grated nutmeg

¼ cup freshly grated Parmesan cheese

1 tablespoon fresh lemon juice

1 tablespoon plain, full-fat Greek yogurt

1 Preheat the oven to 425°F. Place the pumpkin, cut side up, on a parchment-lined baking sheet and brush it with 1 tablespoon of the olive oil. Sprinkle half of the salt over the pumpkin, place it in the oven, and roast for 25 to 30 minutes, until the flesh is tender. Remove from the oven and let the pumpkin cool.

2 When the pumpkin is cool enough to handle, scrape the flesh into a food processor. Add the remaining ingredients and puree until smooth. Taste, adjust the seasoning as necessary, and enjoy.

PAIRS WELL WITH: WHOLE-WHEAT CRACKERS, DARK BREADS, CURED MEATS

COCONUT & CILANTRO
Chutney

YIELD: 6 SERVINGS / **ACTIVE TIME:** 5 MINUTES / **TOTAL TIME:** 5 MINUTES

INGREDIENTS

1 bunch of fresh cilantro

¼ cup grated fresh coconut

15 fresh mint leaves

1 tablespoon minced chile pepper

1 garlic clove

1 teaspoon grated ginger

1 plum tomato, chopped

1 tablespoon fresh lemon juice

Water, as needed

Salt, to taste

1 Place all the ingredients, except for the water and salt, in a food processor and puree until smooth, adding water as needed to get the desired consistency.

2 Taste, season with salt, and chill in the refrigerator until ready to serve.

PAIRS WELL WITH: SPICY FOODS, FLATBREADS, SUMMER-THEMED BOARDS

SMOKED POTATO
Puree

YIELD: 8 SERVINGS / **ACTIVE TIME:** 15 MINUTES / **TOTAL TIME:** 1 HOUR AND 15 MINUTES

INGREDIENTS

½ cup wood chips

2 sweet potatoes, peeled and chopped

1 Yukon Gold potato, peeled and chopped

2 teaspoons kosher salt, plus more to taste

½ cup heavy cream

2 tablespoons unsalted butter

1 Preheat the oven to 250°F. Place the wood chips in a cast-iron skillet and place the pan over high heat. When the wood chips start to smoke, place the skillet in a deep roasting pan. Set the sweet potatoes and potato in the roasting pan (not in the skillet) and cover the roasting pan with aluminum foil. Place in the oven for 30 minutes.

2 While the potatoes are smoking in the oven, bring water to a boil in a large saucepan. Remove the potatoes from the oven, salt the boiling water, and add the potatoes. Cook until they are fork-tender, 20 to 25 minutes. Drain, place in a mixing bowl, and add the remaining ingredients. Mash until smooth, season with salt, and serve immediately.

PAIRS WELL WITH: MILD CHEESES, CRUSTY BREADS, MEDITERRANEAN-THEMED BOARDS

TABBOULEH

YIELD: 4 CUPS / ACTIVE TIME: 15 MINUTES / TOTAL TIME: 45 MINUTES

INGREDIENTS

½ cup bulgur wheat

1½ cups boiling water

½ teaspoon kosher salt, plus more to taste

½ cup fresh lemon juice

2 cups fresh parsley, chopped

2 cucumbers, peeled, seeded, and diced

2 tomatoes, diced

6 scallions, trimmed and sliced

1 cup fresh mint leaves, chopped

2 tablespoons extra-virgin olive oil

Black pepper, to taste

½ cup crumbled feta cheese

1 Place the bulgur in a heatproof bowl and add the boiling water, salt, and half of the lemon juice. Cover and let sit for about 20 minutes, until the bulgur has absorbed the liquid and is tender. Drain excess liquid if necessary. Let the bulgur cool completely.

2 When the bulgur has cooled, add the parsley, cucumbers, tomatoes, scallions, mint, olive oil, pepper, and remaining lemon juice and stir to combine.

3 Top the tabbouleh with the feta and enjoy.

PAIRS WELL WITH: MEDITERRANEAN-THEMED BOARDS, TANGY & SALTY CHEESES, FLATBREADS

BEET
Relish

YIELD: 8 SERVINGS / **ACTIVE TIME:** 15 MINUTES / **TOTAL TIME:** 1 HOUR

INGREDIENTS

4 red beets, trimmed and rinsed well

1 large shallot, minced

2 teaspoons white wine vinegar

Salt and pepper, to taste

1 tablespoon red wine vinegar

2 tablespoons extra-virgin olive oil

1   Preheat the oven to 400°F. Place the beets in a baking dish, add a splash of water, cover the dish with aluminum foil, and place it in the oven. Roast the beets until they are so tender that a knife easily goes to the center when poked, 45 minutes to 1 hour. Remove from the oven, remove the foil, and let the beets cool.

2   While the beets are in the oven, place the shallot and white wine vinegar in a mixing bowl, season the mixture with salt, and stir to combine. Let the mixture marinate.

3   Peel the beets, dice them or slice them thin, and place them in a mixing bowl. Add the remaining ingredients and the shallot mixture, season to taste, and serve.

PAIRS WELL WITH: DARK BREADS, SMOKED SALMON, CRUDITÉS

PECAN

Muhammara

YIELD: 4 SERVINGS / ACTIVE TIME: 15 MINUTES / TOTAL TIME: 30 MINUTES

INGREDIENTS

2 red bell peppers

¼ cup pecans

1 teaspoon kosher salt

1 teaspoon Aleppo pepper

½ cup extra-virgin olive oil

Juice of 1 lemon

1 tablespoon pomegranate molasses

¼ cup bread crumbs

1 tablespoon chopped fresh parsley

1   Warm a cast-iron skillet over medium-high heat. Place the peppers in the pan and cook until they are charred all over, turning them as needed.

2   Place the peppers in a bowl, cover it with plastic wrap, and let them steam for 15 minutes.

3   Peel the peppers, remove the stems and seed pods, and place the peppers in a blender.

4   Add the pecans, salt, Aleppo pepper, olive oil, lemon juice, and molasses and puree until smooth.

5   Add the bread crumbs and fold to incorporate them. Sprinkle the parsley on top and enjoy.

PAIRS WELL WITH: HOLIDAY-THEMED BOARDS, CRUDITÉS, FLATBREADS

HUMMUS

YIELD: 6 SERVINGS / **ACTIVE TIME:** 15 MINUTES / **TOTAL TIME:** 24 HOURS

INGREDIENTS

1 lb. dried chickpeas, soaked overnight

¼ cup extra-virgin olive oil

4 garlic cloves

2 teaspoons kosher salt

Juice of 1½ lemons

1½ cups tahini

1   Drain the chickpeas, place them in a medium saucepan, and cover them with at least 3 inches of water. Boil until tender, 1 to 2 hours. Throw a chickpea against the wall and see if it sticks. When it does, it's ready enough for hummus.

2   Drain the chickpeas and transfer them immediately to a food processor.

3   Puree the chickpeas for 15 seconds. Add the olive oil, garlic, salt, and lemon juice and puree on high until the mixture is smooth, about 2 minutes.

4   Add the tahini and puree until the hummus is creamy, smooth, and thick, about 1 minute. Taste, adjust the seasoning as necessary, and enjoy.

PAIRS WELL WITH: FLATBREADS, CRUDITÉS, MEDITERRANEAN-THEMED BOARDS

RED
Zhug

YIELD: 10 SERVINGS / **ACTIVE TIME:** 10 MINUTES / **TOTAL TIME:** 10 MINUTES

INGREDIENTS

4 Fresno chile peppers, stems removed, chopped

2 cups fresh parsley leaves

1 onion, chopped

5 garlic cloves

Juice of 1 lemon

1 tablespoon kosher salt

1 teaspoon cayenne pepper

1 tablespoon cumin

2 tablespoons paprika

¾ cup extra-virgin olive oil

¼ cup water

1   Place the chiles, parsley, onion, garlic, and lemon juice in a food processor and pulse until the mixture is roughly chopped.

2   Add the salt, cayenne, cumin, and paprika, and, with the food processor running on high, add the olive oil in a slow stream. Add the water as needed until the mixture is smooth.

3   Taste, adjust the seasoning as necessary, and serve.

PAIRS WELL WITH: DUMPLINGS, CREAMY DIPS, MILD CHEESES

PICKLED
Applesauce

YIELD: 8 SERVINGS / ACTIVE TIME: 20 MINUTES / TOTAL TIME: 1 HOUR

INGREDIENTS

3 lbs. Granny Smith apples, peeled and sliced

1 teaspoon cinnamon

Pinch of ground cloves

½ cup sugar

1½ cups white vinegar

1 Place the ingredients in a large saucepan and bring to a boil over high heat.

2 Reduce the heat to medium-high and simmer until the liquid has reduced by one-third. Remove the pan from heat and let it cool to room temperature.

3 Place the mixture in a food processor and puree on high until smooth, about 2 minutes. Serve immediately or store in the refrigerator.

PAIRS WELL WITH: GAME MEATS, DARK BREADS

CUCUMBER, TOMATO &
Mango Relish

YIELD: 10 SERVINGS / **ACTIVE TIME:** 10 MINUTES / **TOTAL TIME:** 10 MINUTES

INGREDIENTS

6 cups halved heirloom cherry tomatoes

4 cups deseeded and diced Persian cucumbers

2 small mangoes, pitted and diced

1 cup diced red onion

2 tablespoons red wine vinegar

¼ cup fresh lemon juice

2 tablespoons za'atar seasoning

1 tablespoon sumac powder

¼ cup fine sea salt, plus more to taste

2 tablespoons black pepper

¼ cup chopped fresh dill

½ cup extra-virgin olive oil

1 Place the ingredients in a large mixing bowl and stir until combined.

2 Taste, adjust the seasoning as necessary, and serve.

PAIRS WELL WITH: CURED MEATS, CRUSTY BREADS, BLUE CHEESES

BABA

Ghanoush

YIELD: 12 SERVINGS / **ACTIVE TIME:** 15 MINUTES / **TOTAL TIME:** 1 HOUR AND 15 MINUTES

INGREDIENTS

2 large eggplants, halved

4 garlic cloves, smashed

4 teaspoons fresh lemon juice, plus more to taste

1½ teaspoons fine sea salt, plus more to taste

½ cup tahini

¼ cup pomegranate arils

¼ cup extra-virgin olive oil

2 teaspoons chopped fresh parsley

1 Preheat the oven to 400°F.

2 Place the eggplants cut side down on a baking sheet, place them in the oven, and roast until they are tender and well browned, about 40 minutes. Remove the eggplants from the oven and let them cool for 10 minutes.

3 Scoop the flesh of the eggplant into a food processor and discard the skins.

4 Add the garlic, lemon juice, salt, and tahini and blitz until the mixture is smooth and creamy, about 1 minute.

5 Taste, adjust the seasoning as necessary, and transfer to a bowl.

6 Top with the pomegranate arils, olive oil, and parsley and enjoy.

PAIRS WELL WITH: NUTS, MEDITERRANEAN-THEMED BOARDS, PICKLED VEGETABLES

LABNEH

YIELD: 8 SERVINGS / **ACTIVE TIME:** 10 MINUTES / **TOTAL TIME:** 2 DAYS

INGREDIENTS

4 cups plain Greek yogurt

½ teaspoon fine sea salt

1 tablespoon extra-virgin olive oil

2 teaspoons za'atar seasoning

1. Place the yogurt in a large bowl and season it with the salt; the salt helps pull out excess whey, giving you a creamier, thicker labneh.

2. Place a fine-mesh strainer on top of a medium-sized bowl. Line the strainer with cheesecloth or a linen towel, letting a few inches hang over the side of the strainer. Spoon the seasoned yogurt into the cheesecloth and gently wrap the sides over the top of the yogurt, protecting it from being exposed to air in the refrigerator.

3. Store everything in the refrigerator for 24 to 48 hours, discarding the whey halfway through if the bowl beneath the strainer becomes too full.

4. Remove the labneh from the cheesecloth and store it in an airtight container.

5. To serve, drizzle the olive oil over the labneh and sprinkle the za'atar on top.

PAIRS WELL WITH: FLATBREADS, DUMPLINGS, SPICY FOODS

LAND
TO SEA

Charcuterie can be as simple as pushing a cart around the grocery store and loading up on various cured meats. But in order to have an answer for every occasion, you have to take some ownership of the carnivore-friendly pieces of your boards. With everything from the spicy and rich to the savory and fresh, these recipes meet that charge.

CHICKEN
Chorizo

YIELD: 4 SERVINGS / **ACTIVE TIME:** 45 MINUTES / **TOTAL TIME:** 24 HOURS

INGREDIENTS

2 oz. guajillo chile peppers

2 oz. pasilla chile peppers

2 boneless, skinless chicken thighs

1 tablespoon annatto seasoning

2 garlic cloves, chopped

1 tablespoon dried thyme

1 tablespoon dried Mexican oregano

1 tablespoon cumin

2 tablespoons smoked paprika

1 teaspoon cayenne pepper

1 teaspoon ground cloves

1 teaspoon onion powder

Salt and pepper, to taste

1   Place the chiles in a heatproof bowl, pour boiling water over them, and let them sit for 30 minutes. Drain and let cool. When cool enough to handle, remove the stems and seeds from the peppers.

2   Grind the chicken thighs in a meat grinder or food processor. Place them in a large mixing bowl, add the chiles and remaining ingredients and stir to combine. Cover with plastic wrap and let the mixture marinate in the refrigerator overnight.

3   You can either leave the chorizo as is, form it into patties, or stuff it into sausage casings. Cook it over medium heat in a large skillet until browned and cooked through, which will be about 8 minutes if left loose or formed into patties, and 12 to 15 minutes if stuffed into sausage casings.

PAIRS WELL WITH: TORTILLA CHIPS, PICKLED VEGETABLES, FRUIT

PROSCIUTTO-WRAPPED
Figs

YIELD: 4 SERVINGS / **ACTIVE TIME:** 10 MINUTES / **TOTAL TIME:** 30 MINUTES

INGREDIENTS

12 thin slices of prosciutto

6 ripe figs, halved lengthwise

Aged balsamic vinegar, to taste

1   Preheat your gas or charcoal grill to high heat (500°F). Wrap the prosciutto tightly around the figs and place them on the grill, cut side down. Cook until browned and crispy all over, 2 to 3 minutes per side.

2   Transfer the figs to a platter, drizzle balsamic vinegar over the top, and serve.

PAIRS WELL WITH: MELON, NUTS, SALTY & BLUE CHEESES

SICILIAN
Meatballs

YIELD: 4 SERVINGS / **ACTIVE TIME:** 20 MINUTES / **TOTAL TIME:** 45 MINUTES

INGREDIENTS

2 tablespoons extra-virgin olive oil

½ small red onion, chopped

2 garlic cloves, minced

1 large egg

2 tablespoons whole milk

½ cup Italian-seasoned bread crumbs

¼ cup freshly grated Parmesan cheese

¼ cup pine nuts, toasted

3 tablespoons minced dried currants

2 teaspoons dried oregano

2 tablespoons chopped fresh parsley

¾ lb. ground pork

½ lb. sweet or spicy ground Italian sausage

Salt and pepper, to taste

1　Preheat the oven to 350°F and line a rimmed baking sheet with aluminum foil.

2　Place the oil in a large skillet and warm over medium-high heat. When it starts to shimmer, add the onion and garlic and cook, stirring frequently, until the onion is translucent, about 3 minutes. Remove the pan from heat and set it aside.

3　Place the egg, milk, bread crumbs, Parmesan, pine nuts, currants, oregano, and parsley in a mixing bowl and stir until combined. Add the pork, sausage, and onion mixture, season with salt and pepper, and stir until thoroughly combined. Working with wet hands, form the mixture into 1½-inch meatballs, arrange them on the baking sheet, and spray the tops with cooking spray.

4　Place the meatballs in the oven and bake until cooked through, about 15 minutes, turning them as necessary. Remove the meatballs from the oven and serve immediately.

PAIRS WELL WITH: ITALIAN- & MEDITERRANEAN-THEMED BOARDS, ROASTED VEGETABLES, CREAMY DIPS

SOUTHWESTERN
Sliders

YIELD: 6 SERVINGS / **ACTIVE TIME:** 20 MINUTES / **TOTAL TIME:** 35 MINUTES

INGREDIENTS

1 large egg

2 chipotle chile peppers in adobo

2 tablespoons whole milk

½ cup bread crumbs

½ cup grated jalapeño jack cheese

3 tablespoons finely chopped fresh cilantro

3 tablespoons canned diced green chiles, drained

4 garlic cloves, minced

1 tablespoon dried oregano

1 tablespoon smoked paprika

2 teaspoons cumin

1¼ lbs. ground beef

Salt and pepper, to taste

6 slider rolls

1 Preheat a gas or charcoal grill to medium heat (450°F). Place the egg, chipotles, milk, and bread crumbs in a food processor and puree until smooth. Place the mixture in a mixing bowl, add the cheese, cilantro, green chiles, garlic, oregano, paprika, and cumin and stir until thoroughly combined.

2 Stir in the beef and season the mixture with salt and pepper. Working with wet hands, form the mixture into 3-inch patties. Place the sliders on the grill and cook until cooked through, about 10 minutes. Remove from the grill, transfer to a platter, and tent loosely with aluminum foil.

3 Let the sliders rest for 10 minutes before sandwiching them between the slider rolls along with your favorite burger fixings.

PAIRS WELL WITH: CREAMY & SPICY CONDIMENTS, SHARP CHEESES

CHICHARRON

YIELD: 6 SERVINGS / ACTIVE TIME: 25 MINUTES / TOTAL TIME: 1 HOUR AND 30 MINUTES

INGREDIENTS

1 lb. pork belly, cut into 1-inch-wide and 6-inch-long strips

1½ tablespoons kosher salt

4 cups lard or canola oil

1 Place a cooling rack in a rimmed baking sheet. Season the pork belly with the salt and let it sit for 15 minutes.

2 Place the lard in a Dutch oven (make sure it doesn't reach more than halfway up the sides of the pot) and warm over medium-high heat. Add the pork belly and cook until golden brown and crispy, about 1 hour.

3 Place the pork belly on the cooling rack and let it drain. When the pork is cool enough to handle, chop it into bite-size pieces and enjoy.

PAIRS WELL WITH: CHOCOLATES, MILD CHEESES, SALSAS & SPICY DIPS

FOIE GRAS
Torchon

YIELD: 4 SERVINGS / ACTIVE TIME: 15 MINUTES / TOTAL TIME: 16 HOURS AND 15 MINUTES

INGREDIENTS

1 lb. foie gras

2 cups whole milk

2 teaspoons kosher salt

2 teaspoons sugar

⅛ teaspoon pink curing salt

1 tablespoon bourbon

1   Place the foie gras in a baking pan, cover it with the milk, and let it soak in the refrigerator for at least 8 hours and up to 24.

2   Strain, and then pass the foie gras through a fine-mesh sieve into a mixing bowl. Stir in the kosher salt, sugar, curing salt, and bourbon and roll the mixture into a log. Wrap the log in cheesecloth and chill in the refrigerator for 8 hours.

3   Unwrap the torchon, slice it, and let the torchon come to room temperature before serving.

PAIRS WELL WITH: DRIED FRUIT, DARK BREADS, POTATO CHIPS

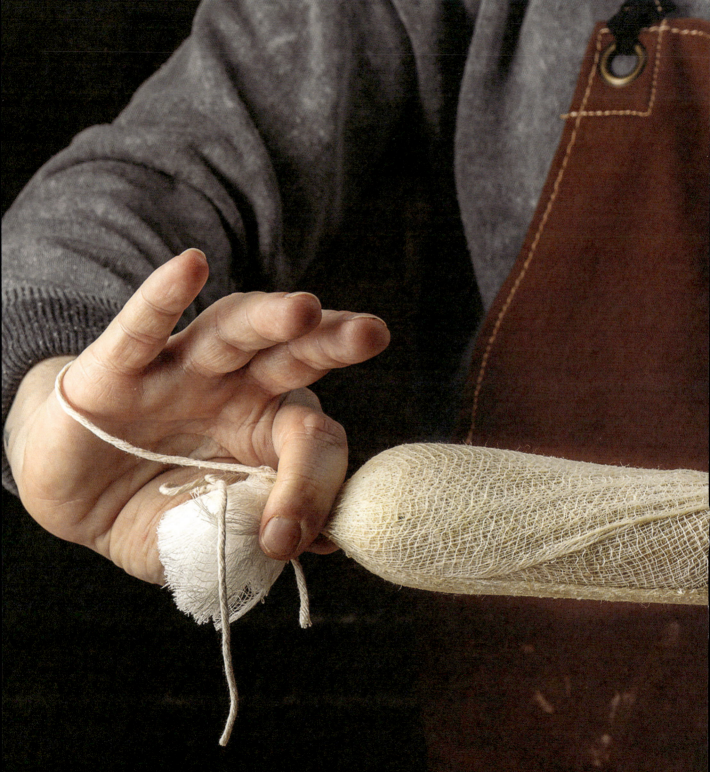

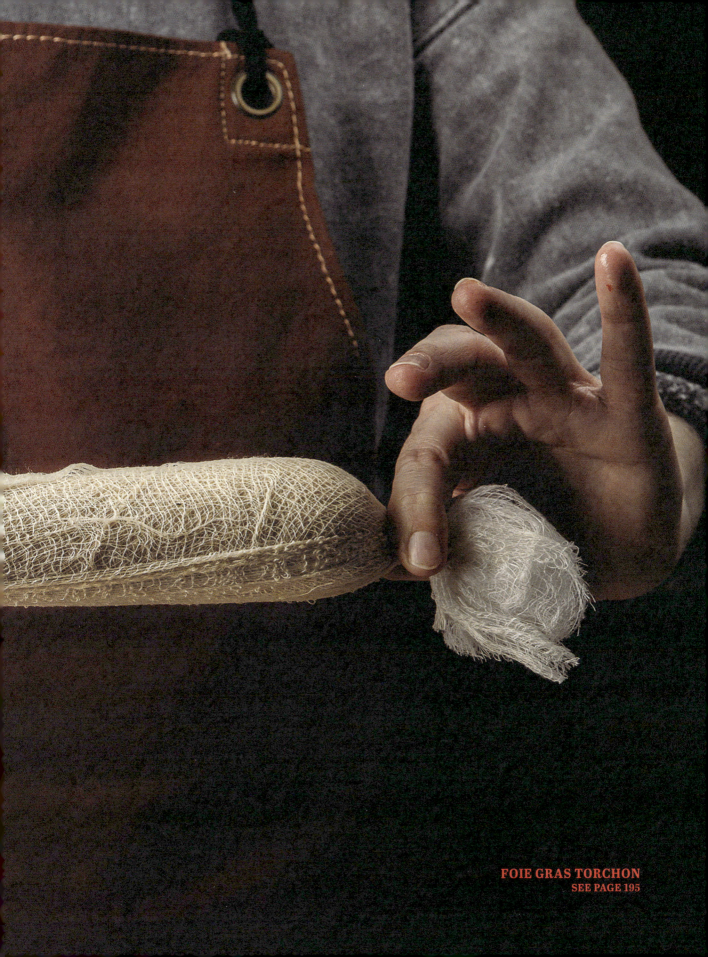

FOIE GRAS TORCHON
SEE PAGE 195

BEEF

Carpaccio

YIELD: 2 SERVINGS / **ACTIVE TIME:** 20 MINUTES / **TOTAL TIME:** 1 HOUR AND 20 MINUTES

INGREDIENTS

4 oz. beef tenderloin

Salt and pepper, to taste

1 tablespoon extra-virgin olive oil

1 Tie the tenderloin with kitchen twine so that it will maintain its shape while it sears. Season the beef with salt and pepper.

2 Coat a skillet with the olive oil and warm it over medium-high heat. Cook, turning it as it browns, until it is seared all over. Remove the tenderloin from the pan and let it cool to room temperature.

3 Cover the tenderloin tightly with plastic wrap and freeze it for 1 hour.

4 To serve, slice the tenderloin as thin as possible and arrange the slices on a plate.

PAIRS WELL WITH: SHARP & NUTTY CHEESES, GARLICKY DIPS & SPREADS, SPRING-THEMED BOARDS

LAMB
Meatballs

YIELD: 4 SERVINGS / **ACTIVE TIME:** 20 MINUTES / **TOTAL TIME:** 40 MINUTES

INGREDIENTS

1 lb. ground lamb

1 white onion, grated

½ cup bread crumbs

1 egg

2 garlic cloves, minced

¼ cup fresh parsley, chopped

¼ cup fresh cilantro, chopped

¾ teaspoon cayenne pepper

¼ teaspoon red pepper flakes

Salt and pepper, to taste

2 tablespoons extra-virgin olive oil

1   Place all the ingredients, except for the olive oil, in a mixing bowl and work the mixture with your hands until combined. Form the mixture into 1-inch meatballs and chill them in the freezer for 15 minutes.

2   Place the olive oil in a large skillet and warm it over medium heat. When the oil starts to shimmer, add the meatballs to the pan and cook, turning occasionally, until they are browned all over and cooked through, about 12 minutes. Let the meatballs cool slightly before serving.

PAIRS WELL WITH: MEDITERRANEAN-THEMED BOARDS, MILD CHEESES, CREAMY & HERBAL CONDIMENTS

CHICKEN
Sausage

YIELD: 4 SERVINGS / **ACTIVE TIME:** 30 MINUTES / **TOTAL TIME:** 1 HOUR

INGREDIENTS

1 boneless, skinless chicken breast, cubed

Salt and pepper, to taste

1 cup heavy cream

¼ cup pistachio meats, chopped

¼ cup dried apricots, chopped

¼ cup raisins, chopped

1   Season the chicken breast with salt and pepper, place it in a food processor, and blitz until it is a smooth puree, about 5 minutes.

2   With the food processor running, add the heavy cream in a steady stream and blitz the puree for another 2 minutes.

3   Transfer the puree to a mixing bowl, add the remaining ingredients, and fold until the nuts and fruits are evenly distributed. Divide the mixture into three portions, roll them into logs, and wrap each one in plastic wrap as tightly as possible. Tie the ends with kitchen twine and poke a few fine holes through the plastic and into the logs with a needle.

4   Prepare an ice bath. Bring water to a steady simmer in a medium saucepan, making sure it does not come to a boil. Place the logs, keeping them in the plastic wrap, in the pan and poach them until their internal temperature reaches 165°F, about 15 minutes.

5   Remove the sausages from the water and submerge them in the ice bath until completely cool. Chill in the refrigerator until ready to serve.

PAIRS WELL WITH: NUTS, SPICY DIPS & CONDIMENTS, FRUIT

PROSCIUTTO &
Cantaloupe Pops

YIELD: 4 SERVINGS / **ACTIVE TIME:** 10 MINUTES / **TOTAL TIME:** 10 MINUTES

INGREDIENTS

2 cups chopped cantaloupe

4 oz. prosciutto, chopped

1   Wrap each piece of cantaloupe in a piece of prosciutto and insert a toothpick or a wooden dowel in the bottom of the piece of cantaloupe. Repeat with the remaining cantaloupe and prosciutto and enjoy.

PAIRS WELL WITH: NUTS, SALTY CHEESES, SUMMER-THEMED BOARDS

CRISPY
Pancetta

YIELD: 4 SERVINGS / **ACTIVE TIME:** 10 MINUTES / **TOTAL TIME:** 40 MINUTES

INGREDIENTS

3 oz. pancetta, sliced

1   Preheat the oven to 350°F and line two baking sheets with silpat mats. Divide the pancetta between the baking sheets.

2   Place the sheets in the oven and bake the pancetta until it is browned and crispy, about 20 minutes. Remove from the oven, transfer the pancetta to a piece of parchment paper, and let cool before serving.

PAIRS WELL WITH: NUTS, FRUIT, ROASTED VEGETABLES

BEEF
Tataki

YIELD: 4 SERVINGS / ACTIVE TIME: 20 MINUTES / TOTAL TIME: 1 HOUR AND 30 MINUTES

INGREDIENTS

8 oz. beef tenderloin

Salt and pepper, to taste

1 tablespoon extra-virgin olive oil, plus more as needed

Juice of 1 orange

2 garlic cloves, minced

1 teaspoon sugar

1 teaspoon grated fresh ginger

1 teaspoon Dijon mustard

1　Cut the tenderloin in half and tie each piece with kitchen twine so that it will maintain its shape while being seared. Season the tenderloin with salt and pepper.

2　Coat the bottom of a large skillet with olive oil and warm it over medium-high heat. Place the tenderloin in the pan and cook, turning the pieces as they brown. Remove the beef from the pan and let it cool to room temperature.

3　Place the remaining ingredients in a bowl and stir to combine. Add the tenderloins and let them marinate for at least 1 hour before slicing and serving.

PAIRS WELL WITH: BLUE CHEESES, PICKLED VEGETABLES, TOAST POINTS (SEE PAGE 52)

VENISON

Jerky

INGREDIENTS

8 oz. venison tri-tip, sliced thin

1 tablespoon soy sauce

1 teaspoon distilled white vinegar

1 teaspoon sesame oil

½ teaspoon honey

¼ teaspoon onion powder

¼ teaspoon minced garlic

⅛ teaspoon grated fresh ginger

1 Place all the ingredients in a mixing bowl and stir to combine. Let the venison marinate for 1 hour.

2 Place the venison on parchment-lined baking sheets, place them in a food dehydrator, and dehydrate at 140°F for 6 to 8 hours. When it is ready, the jerky should have lost about one-third of its weight and have a slightly bouncy texture.

PAIRS WELL WITH: DARK BREADS, TART CONDIMENTS, SWEET & BUTTERY CHEESES

DUCK

Rillette

YIELD: 4 SERVINGS / **ACTIVE TIME:** 15 MINUTES / **TOTAL TIME:** 3 HOURS

INGREDIENTS

6 duck legs

Salt and pepper, to taste

2 tablespoons extra-virgin olive oil

¾ cup duck fat

½ cup fresh parsley, chopped

6 tablespoons unsalted butter, melted and cooled slightly

1   Pat the duck legs dry with paper towels and season them generously with salt. With the tip of a knife, gently poke the skin all around each leg. This will help release the fat as it renders. Let the legs rest at room temperature for at least 25 minutes.

2   Coat the bottom of a Dutch oven with the olive oil, add the duck legs, and set the oven to 285°F. Place the Dutch oven, uncovered, in the oven. You do not want to preheat the oven, as starting the duck at a low temperature allows its fat to render. After 1½ hours, check the duck. It should be under a layer of duck fat and the skin should be getting crisp. If the legs aren't browned and crispy, let the duck cook longer. When the skin is starting to crisp, raise the oven's temperature to 375°F and cook the duck for another 15 minutes.

3   Remove the pot from the oven, remove the duck legs from the fat, and let them rest for 10 minutes.

4   Remove the meat from the duck legs and finely chop it. Place the meat in a mixing bowl.

5   Add the duck fat and parsley, fold to combine, and season the mixture with salt and pepper.

6   Place the mixture in a jar, top it with the melted butter, and refrigerate until ready to serve. The rillette will keep in the refrigerator for 5 to 7 days.

PAIRS WELL WITH: CROSTINI (SEE PAGE 51), NUTTY CHEESES, DEVILED EGGS

POPCORN Chicken

YIELD: 4 SERVINGS / ACTIVE TIME: 25 MINUTES / TOTAL TIME: 1 HOUR AND 30 MINUTES

INGREDIENTS

3 garlic cloves, smashed

1 egg white

1 tablespoon soy sauce

1½ tablespoons sesame oil

½ teaspoon white pepper

1 tablespoon cornstarch

Salt, to taste

1 lb. boneless, skin-on chicken breast, cut into bite-size pieces

7 tablespoons tapioca starch, plus more as needed

2 cups canola oil

1   Place the garlic, egg white, soy sauce, sesame oil, white pepper, cornstarch, and salt in a mixing bowl and stir to combine. Add the chicken, toss to coat, and cover the bowl. Chill in the refrigerator for 1 hour.

2   Dust a sheet pan with tapioca starch, add the chicken, and turn it in the starch until it is coated, adding more tapioca starch as necessary.

3   Place the canola oil in a Dutch oven and warm it to 350°F over medium heat. Shake the chicken to remove any excess starch, add it to the pot in batches, and fry until golden brown. Make sure you do not overcrowd the pot.

4   Place the cooked chicken on a paper towel–lined plate to drain and briefly let it cool before serving.

PAIRS WELL WITH: SPICY DIPS, SUMMER-THEMED BOARDS, FRUIT

MUFFULETTA

YIELD: 4 TO 6 SERVINGS / **ACTIVE TIME:** 45 MINUTES / **TOTAL TIME:** 24 HOURS

INGREDIENTS

1 red bell pepper

1 cup sun-dried tomatoes in olive oil, drained and chopped

1 cup pitted green olives, chopped

1 cup pitted black olives, chopped

¼ cup extra-virgin olive oil

¼ cup chopped fresh parsley

2 tablespoons fresh lemon juice

1 teaspoon dried oregano

1 loaf of Italian or French bread, halved lengthwise

2 cups torn lettuce

4 oz. mortadella, sliced thin

4 oz. provolone cheese, sliced thin

4 oz. soppressata, sliced thin

1   Preheat the oven to 400°F. Place the bell pepper on a baking sheet, place it in the oven, and roast, turning it occasionally, until it is charred all over, about 25 minutes. Remove the pepper from the oven and let it cool. When cool enough to handle, remove the charred flesh, chop the pepper, and discard the seed pod and stem. Place the roasted pepper in a mixing bowl.

2   Add the tomatoes, olives, oil, parsley, lemon juice, and oregano to the bowl. Cover and refrigerate overnight.

3   Drain the olive mixture and reserve the liquid. Remove most of the crumb from one of the halves of the bread and generously brush the cut sides with the reserved liquid. Fill the piece of bread with the crumb removed with half of the olive mixture and top with half of the lettuce and all the mortadella, provolone, and soppressata.

4   Layer the remaining lettuce over the soppressata and top with the remaining olive mixture and the other piece of bread. Wrap the sandwich in plastic wrap and place it on a large plate. Place another plate on top and weigh it down with a good-sized cookbook or something similar. Refrigerate for at least 1 hour before slicing and serving.

PAIRS WELL WITH: OLIVES, MILD CHEESES, FOOTBALL TAILGATE-THEMED BOARDS

CHICKEN 65

YIELD: 6 SERVINGS / **ACTIVE TIME:** 1 HOUR / **TOTAL TIME:** 2 HOURS

INGREDIENTS

1 lb. boneless, skinless chicken thighs, chopped

1 teaspoon mashed fresh ginger

1 garlic clove, minced

½ teaspoon chili powder, plus more to taste

1 teaspoon fresh lemon juice

½ teaspoon black pepper, plus more to taste

⅛ teaspoon turmeric

Salt, to taste

2 tablespoons cornstarch

1 tablespoon rice flour

Canola oil, as needed

½ teaspoon sugar

2 tablespoons plain yogurt

1 tablespoon unsalted butter

3 to 5 curry leaves

2 green chile peppers, stems and seeds removed, chopped

½ teaspoon cumin

1 Rinse the chicken and pat it dry. Place the ginger, one-third of the garlic, the chili powder, lemon juice, black pepper, turmeric, and salt in a mixing bowl and stir to combine. Add the chicken and stir to coat. Place it in the refrigerator and marinate for at least 1 hour.

2 When ready to cook the chicken, place the cornstarch and flour in a mixing bowl, stir to combine, and dredge the marinated chicken in the mixture.

3 Add canola oil to a Dutch oven until it is 2 inches deep and warm it to 350°F over medium heat.

4 Place the sugar, remaining garlic, and yogurt in a mixing bowl, season with chili powder and salt, and stir to combine. Set the mixture aside.

5 Working in batches if necessary to avoid crowding the pot, place the chicken in the oil and fry until golden brown and cooked through. Remove the cooked chicken from the pot and let it drain on a paper towel–lined plate.

6 Place the butter, curry leaves, chiles, and cumin in a small pan and sauté over medium heat until fragrant. Stir in the yogurt mixture and bring the sauce to a simmer. Add the fried chicken to the sauce and cook until the chicken has absorbed most of the liquid. Let cool briefly before serving.

PAIRS WELL WITH: CREAMY CONDIMENTS, PICKLED VEGETABLES, NUTS

KEFTA

YIELD: 4 SERVINGS / **ACTIVE TIME:** 35 MINUTES / **TOTAL TIME:** 1 HOUR

INGREDIENTS

1½ lbs. ground lamb

½ lb. ground beef

½ white onion, minced

2 garlic cloves, roasted and mashed

Zest of 1 lemon

1 cup fresh parsley, chopped

2 tablespoons chopped fresh mint

1 teaspoon cinnamon

2 tablespoons cumin

1 tablespoon paprika

1 teaspoon coriander

Salt and pepper, to taste

¼ cup extra-virgin olive oil

1 Place all the ingredients, except for the olive oil, in a mixing bowl and stir until well combined. Place a small bit of the mixture in a skillet and cook over medium heat until cooked through. Taste and adjust the seasoning in the remaining mixture as necessary. Working with wet hands, form the mixture into 18 ovals and place three meatballs on each skewer.

2 Place the olive oil in a Dutch oven and warm it over medium-high heat. Working in batches, add three skewers to the pot and sear the kefta until browned all over and nearly cooked through. Transfer the browned kefta to a paper towel–lined plate to drain.

3 When all the kefta have been browned, return all of the skewers to the pot, cover it, and remove from heat. Let stand for 10 minutes so the kefta get cooked through.

4 When the kefta are cooked through, remove them from the skewers and serve.

PAIRS WELL WITH: MEDITERRANEAN-THEMED BOARDS, ROASTED VEGETABLES, CREAMY DIPS

CORN
Dogs

YIELD: 4 SERVINGS / **ACTIVE TIME:** 20 MINUTES / **TOTAL TIME:** 1 HOUR

INGREDIENTS

1 cup cornmeal

1 cup all-purpose flour

2 teaspoons kosher salt

¼ cup sugar

4 teaspoons baking powder

1 egg white

1 cup milk

Canola oil, as needed

4 hot dogs

1   Soak four bamboo skewers in water for 30 minutes. Place the cornmeal, flour, salt, sugar, and baking powder in a mixing bowl and stir to combine. Place the egg white and milk in a separate bowl and whisk to combine. Add the wet mixture to the dry mixture and stir until thoroughly combined.

2   Add oil to a Dutch oven until it is approximately 2 inches deep and warm it to 350°F over medium heat. Thread the hot dogs onto the skewers and roll them in the batter until well coated. When the oil is at the correct temperature, add the corn dogs and fry until golden brown, about 3 minutes.

PAIRS WELL WITH: SUMMER-THEMED BOARDS, SPICY DIPS, PICKLED VEGETABLES

SHRIMP IN
Adobo

YIELD: 4 SERVINGS / ACTIVE TIME: 30 MINUTES / TOTAL TIME: 45 MINUTES

INGREDIENTS

4 guajillo chile peppers, stemmed and seeded

6 garlic cloves

2 small Roma tomatoes

3 tablespoons chopped chipotles in adobo

Salt, to taste

1 lb. large shrimp, shelled and deveined

¼ cup lard

1   Place the dried chiles in a dry skillet and toast over medium heat until they darken and become fragrant and pliable. Submerge them in a bowl of hot water and let them soak for 15 to 20 minutes.

2   Drain the chiles and reserve the soaking liquid. Add the chiles to a blender along with the garlic, tomatoes, chipotles, and a small amount of the soaking liquid and puree until the mixture is a smooth paste. Season the adobo marinade with salt and let it cool completely.

3   Place the shrimp in the adobo and marinate for at least 20 to 30 minutes.

4   Place some of the lard in a large skillet and warm it over medium-high heat. Working in batches if needed to avoid crowding the pan, add the shrimp and cook until they are just firm and turn pink, about 2 minutes. Add more lard to the pan if it starts to look dry. Serve immediately.

PAIRS WELL WITH: TORTILLA CHIPS, SUMMER-THEMED BOARDS

SMOKED

Oysters

YIELD: 4 SERVINGS / **ACTIVE TIME:** 30 MINUTES / **TOTAL TIME:** 45 MINUTES

INGREDIENTS

1 bunch of green allspice leaves or bay leaves

12 oysters, rinsed and scrubbed

1 small bunch of banana leaves

7 tablespoons extra-virgin olive oil

7 tablespoons fresh lime juice

3 serrano chile peppers, stemmed, seeded, and minced

1 cup fresh cilantro stems, chopped

1 Preheat a charcoal grill to medium-high heat (about 450°F). When the grill is hot and the coals are glowing and covered with a thin layer of ash, place a grill rack on top of the coals and cover the rack with the allspice leaves. Place the closed oysters on top and the cover with the banana leaves. The leaves will begin to smolder and then catch fire. After 3 to 4 minutes, the oysters will begin to open and absorb the smoke. Using tongs, carefully remove the oysters and arrange them on a platter or serving board.

2 Place the olive oil, lime juice, chiles, and cilantro in a bowl and stir until thoroughly combined. Serve this sauce alongside the oysters.

PAIRS WELL WITH: MIGNONETTE SAUCE, SUMMER-THEMED BOARDS, PICKLED VEGETABLES

SMOKED OYSTERS
SEE PAGE 225

AGUACHILE
Verde

YIELD: 4 SERVINGS / **ACTIVE TIME:** 10 MINUTES / **TOTAL TIME:** 20 MINUTES

INGREDIENTS

1¾ cups fresh lime juice

3 serrano chile peppers, stemmed and seeded

1 cup fresh cilantro, chopped, plus more for garnish

3 tablespoons extra-virgin olive oil

2 tablespoons apple juice

1 teaspoon honey

Salt, to taste

1 lb. shrimp, shelled and deveined; or scallops, feet removed, rinsed

¼ red onion, julienned

1 cucumber, sliced

Flesh of 1 avocado, diced

1   Place the lime juice, serrano peppers, cilantro, olive oil, apple juice, and honey in a blender and puree until smooth. Season the aguachile with salt and set it aside.

2   Slice the shrimp in half lengthwise and place them in a shallow bowl. Cover with the red onion, cucumber, and avocado.

3   Pour the aguachile over the shrimp and let the mixture macerate for 5 to 10 minutes before enjoying.

PAIRS WELL WITH: SPICY FOODS, TORTILLA CHIPS

MASA-CRUSTED
Sardines

YIELD: 2 SERVINGS / **ACTIVE TIME:** 10 MINUTES / **TOTAL TIME:** 30 MINUTES

INGREDIENTS

8 oz. sardines, cleaned and heads removed

Salt, to taste

1 cup masa harina

¼ cup all-purpose flour

1 teaspoon cumin

1 teaspoon coriander

½ teaspoon ground cloves

1 teaspoon allspice

1 teaspoon ginger

1 teaspoon paprika

2 cups extra-virgin olive oil

1   Rinse the sardines and pat them dry with a paper towel. Season lightly with salt.

2   Place the masa harina, flour, and half of the seasonings in a mixing bowl and stir to combine.

3   Dredge the sardines in the masa mixture until completely coated. Set them on paper towels and let them rest for 5 minutes. The resting period allows the sardines to release a bit of moisture, which will help more of the masa stick to them, producing a lighter and crispier result.

4   After 5 minutes, dredge the sardines in the masa mixture again until coated.

5   Place the olive oil in a deep skillet and warm it to 325°F. Working in batches, gently slip the sardines into the oil and fry them until crispy and golden brown, about 4 minutes, turning them over once. Place the fried sardines on a paper towel–lined plate to drain, sprinkle the remaining seasonings over them, and enjoy.

PAIRS WELL WITH: PICKLED VEGETABLES, SPICY FOODS, MEXICAN-STYLE LAGERS

BEET-CURED
Salmon

YIELD: 4 SERVINGS / **ACTIVE TIME:** 30 MINUTES / **TOTAL TIME:** 16 HOURS

INGREDIENTS

2 cups chopped beets

1 cup kosher salt

½ cup sugar

1 cup water

1 lb. salmon, skin removed
and deboned

1   Place the beets, salt, and sugar in a food processor and pulse until the beets
are finely chopped. Add the water in a slow stream and pulse until the mixture is a smooth puree.

2   Place the salmon in a baking dish and pour the puree over it. Place the
salmon in the refrigerator and let it cure for at least 12 hours.

3   Rinse the salmon under cold water. Place it on a wire rack set in a rimmed
baking sheet and let it dry, uncovered, in the refrigerator for 4 hours before
serving.

PAIRS WELL WITH: CREAMY DIPS, PICKLED VEGETABLES, BREAKFAST & BRUNCH BOARDS

CHARRED
Octopus

YIELD: 8 SERVINGS / **ACTIVE TIME:** 20 MINUTES / **TOTAL TIME:** 2 HOURS

INGREDIENTS

1 whole octopus, frozen

Extra-virgin olive oil, as needed

1   Fill a pot, large enough to fully submerge the octopus under water, with water and bring it to a simmer. Add the octopus and cover the pot. Simmer until the octopus is very tender, 45 minutes to 1 hour. Remove the tentacles from the octopus and let them cool.

2   Warm a cast-iron skillet over high heat. Brush the pan with some olive oil, pat the octopus tentacles dry, and sear them until slightly charred. Serve immediately.

PAIRS WELL WITH: PICKLED VEGETABLES, HERB-BASED CONDIMENTS, AIOLI

SWORDFISH
Crudo

YIELD: 4 SERVINGS / **ACTIVE TIME:** 15 MINUTES / **TOTAL TIME:** 30 MINUTES

INGREDIENTS

4 oz. sushi-grade swordfish

Salt, to taste

1 teaspoon freshly cracked black pepper

Juice of ½ lemon

1 tablespoon extra-virgin olive oil

1 tablespoon sliced scallions

4 slices of jalapeño chile pepper

3 slices of tomato

1   Chill a plate in the refrigerator for 10 minutes.

2   Slice the swordfish thin against the grain and arrange the slices on the chilled plate, making sure not to overlap the pieces.

3   Season the fish generously with salt, then sprinkle the pepper and lemon juice over it. Drizzle the olive oil over the top and sprinkle the scallions over the fish.

4   Arrange the jalapeño and tomato on the side of the plate and chill in the refrigerator until ready to serve.

PAIRS WELL WITH: SUMMER- & MEDITERRANEAN-THEMED BOARDS, OLIVES

SHRIMP
Cocktail

YIELD: 4 SERVINGS / **ACTIVE TIME:** 20 MINUTES / **TOTAL TIME:** 1 HOUR

INGREDIENTS

½ cup ketchup

2 tablespoons horseradish

2 tablespoons Worcestershire sauce

Juice of ½ lemon

1 teaspoon Old Bay seasoning

8 oz. large shrimp, shelled and deveined

1　Place the ketchup, horseradish, Worcestershire sauce, and lemon juice in a bowl, stir to combine, and chill in the refrigerator for 1 hour.

2　Prepare an ice bath. Place water in a medium saucepan and bring it to a boil. Add the Old Bay and the shrimp and poach the shrimp until cooked through, about 4 minutes.

3　Shock the shrimp in the ice water and chill in the refrigerator until ready to serve.

PAIRS WELL WITH: SUMMER-THEMED BOARDS, SPARKLING WINES, POTATO CHIPS

DUMPLINGS & OTHER DECADENT BITES

No one can quite define what is and what is not
a dumpling, but this much is clear: they are delicious, and
are wonderful on a charcuterie board, contained and delectable
little nuggets that entice all comers. If a dumpling isn't going to hit
the mark, there's also a dozen or so similarly rich offerings
that will put a smile on everyone's face.

EMPANADAS

YIELD: 4 SERVINGS / **ACTIVE TIME:** 30 MINUTES / **TOTAL TIME:** 1 HOUR AND 45 MINUTES

INGREDIENTS

For the Dough

¼ teaspoon kosher salt

6 tablespoons warm water (110°F)

1½ cups all-purpose flour, plus more as needed

3 tablespoons lard or unsalted butter, cut into small pieces

For the Filling

2 teaspoons extra-virgin olive oil

1 yellow onion, minced

1 garlic clove, minced

¾ lb. ground pork

1 (14 oz.) can of crushed tomatoes

½ teaspoon kosher salt

¼ teaspoon black pepper

1 cinnamon stick, chopped

2 whole cloves

2 tablespoons raisins

2 teaspoons apple cider vinegar

2 tablespoons slivered almonds, toasted

Canola oil, as needed

1 To prepare the dough, dissolve the salt in the warm water. Place the flour in a mixing bowl, add the lard or butter, and work the mixture with a pastry blender until it is coarse crumbs. Add the salted water and knead the mixture until a stiff dough forms. Cut the dough into eight pieces, cover them with plastic wrap, and chill in the refrigerator for 20 minutes.

2 To prepare the filling, place the olive oil in a skillet and warm over medium heat. When the oil starts to shimmer, add the onion and cook until it has softened, about 5 minutes. Add the garlic, cook for 2 minutes, and then add the ground pork. Cook, breaking it up, until it is light brown, about 5 minutes. Drain off any excess fat and add the tomatoes, salt, pepper, cinnamon stick, cloves, raisins, and vinegar. Simmer until the filling is thick, about 30 minutes. Remove from heat and let cool before folding in the toasted almonds.

3 Add canola oil to a Dutch oven until it is 2 inches deep and bring it to 350°F. Preheat the oven to 200°F and place a platter in the oven.

4 Place the pieces of dough on a flour-dusted work surface and roll each one into a 5-inch circle. Place 3 tablespoons of the filling in the center of one circle, brush the edge with water, and fold into a half-moon. Crimp the edge to seal the empanada tight, pressing down on the filling to remove as much air as possible. Repeat with the remaining filling and pieces of dough.

5 Working in two batches, place the empanadas in the hot oil and fry until golden brown, about 5 minutes. Drain the cooked empanadas on paper towels and place them in the warm oven while you cook the next batch.

PAIRS WELL WITH: CREAMY & HERB-BASED DIPS, SMOKED MEATS

CRAB

Rangoon

YIELD: 6 SERVINGS / ACTIVE TIME: 25 MINUTES / TOTAL TIME: 45 MINUTES

INGREDIENTS

1 lb. cream cheese, softened

6 oz. fresh crabmeat

2 tablespoons confectioners' sugar

¼ teaspoon kosher salt

40 wonton wrappers

Canola oil, as needed

1   Place the cream cheese, crabmeat, sugar, and salt in a medium bowl and fold until the mixture is combined.

2   Place 1 tablespoon of the mixture in the middle of a wrapper. Rub the wrapper's edge with a wet finger, bring the corners together, pinch to seal tightly, and transfer to a parchment-lined baking sheet. Repeat with the remaining wrappers and filling.

3   Add oil to a Dutch oven until it is 2 inches deep and warm it to 325°F over medium heat. Working in batches, gently slip the wontons into the hot oil and fry, while turning, until golden all over, about 3 minutes. Transfer the cooked dumplings to a paper towel–lined wire rack and let cool briefly before serving.

PAIRS WELL WITH: SWEET & SPICY SAUCES, SUMMER-THEMED BOARDS, DRY WHITE WINES

TAKOYAKI

YIELD: 4 SERVINGS / ACTIVE TIME: 20 MINUTES / TOTAL TIME: 20 MINUTES

INGREDIENTS

2 teaspoons sake

2 teaspoons mirin

2 teaspoons soy sauce

2 teaspoons oyster sauce

2 teaspoons Worcestershire sauce

1 tablespoon sugar

1 tablespoon ketchup

Salt and white pepper, to taste

2 tablespoons water, plus more as needed

1 large egg

1½ cups chicken stock

¾ cup all-purpose flour

1 cup minced cooked octopus

2 scallion greens, sliced thin

¼ cup minced pickled ginger

1 Place the sake, mirin, soy sauce, oyster sauce, Worcestershire sauce, sugar, ketchup, salt, and white pepper in a mixing bowl and stir to combine. Set the mixture aside.

2 Place the water, egg, and stock in a bowl and stir until combined. Sprinkle the flour over the mixture and stir until all the flour has been incorporated and the mixture is a thick batter. Add the sake-and-mirin mixture and stir to incorporate. Pour the batter into a measuring cup with a spout.

3 Coat the wells of an aebleskiver pan or a muffin pan with nonstick cooking spray and place it over medium heat. When the pan is hot, fill the wells of the pan halfway with the batter and add a pinch of octopus, scallion, and pickled ginger to each. Fill the wells the rest of the way with the batter, until they are almost overflowing.

4 Cook the dumplings for approximately 2 minutes and use a chopstick to flip each one over. Turn the fritters as needed until they are golden brown on both sides and piping hot. Enjoy immediately.

PAIRS WELL WITH: LIGHT LAGERS, SUMMER-THEMED BOARDS, SWEET & SAVORY SAUCES

ARANCINI

YIELD: 8 SERVINGS / ACTIVE TIME: 30 MINUTES / TOTAL TIME: 1 HOUR AND 30 MINUTES

INGREDIENTS

5 cups chicken stock

8 tablespoons unsalted butter

2 cups Arborio rice

1 small white onion, grated

1 cup white wine

4 oz. Fontina cheese, grated

Salt and pepper, to taste

Canola oil, as needed

6 large eggs, beaten

5 cups panko

1 Bring the stock to a simmer in a large saucepan. In a skillet, melt the butter over high heat. Once the butter is foaming, add the rice and onion and cook until the rice has a toasty fragrance, about 4 minutes. Deglaze the skillet with the white wine and cook until the wine has almost completely been absorbed. Then, reduce the heat to medium-high and begin adding the stock ¼ cup at a time, stirring until it has been incorporated. Continue adding the stock until the rice is al dente.

2 Turn off the heat, stir in the cheese, and season the risotto with salt and pepper. Pour it onto a baking sheet and let cool.

3 Add the oil to a Dutch oven until it is 2 inches deep and warm over medium heat until it reaches 350°F. When the rice mixture is cool, form it into golf ball–sized spheres. Dredge them in the eggs and then the panko until coated all over. Place the balls in the oil and cook until warmed through and golden brown. Transfer to a paper towel–lined plate to drain and let cool slightly before enjoying.

PAIRS WELL WITH: PICKLED VEGETABLES, CURED MEATS, CREAMY DIPS

MAPLE
Walnuts

YIELD: 2 CUPS / **ACTIVE TIME:** 15 MINUTES / **TOTAL TIME:** 45 MINUTES

INGREDIENTS

1 tablespoon unsalted butter

⅓ cup real maple syrup

⅛ teaspoon kosher salt

2 cups walnut halves

1. Preheat the oven to 375°F and line a baking sheet with parchment paper.

2. Place the butter in a skillet and melt it over medium heat. Stir in the maple syrup and salt and simmer until the mixture is frothy, about 3 minutes.

3. Add the walnuts and stir to coat. Cook, stirring, for about 3 minutes.

4. Transfer the walnuts to the baking sheet, place them in the oven, and bake until caramelized, about 10 minutes. Remove, stir, and let cool until the maple glaze hardens, about 30 minutes.

PAIRS WELL WITH: AUTUMN-THEMED BOARDS, CURED MEATS, BOLD CHEESES

ROASTED

Chestnuts

YIELD: 8 SERVINGS / ACTIVE TIME: 5 MINUTES / TOTAL TIME: 1 HOUR

INGREDIENTS

1 lb. chestnuts

½ teaspoon kosher salt

¼ teaspoon black pepper

2 tablespoons unsalted butter, melted

1 tablespoon extra-virgin olive oil

3 sprigs of fresh thyme

1 cinnamon stick

2 whole cloves

1   Preheat the oven to 425°F. Carve an "X" on the rounded side of each chestnut and place them in a bowl of hot water. Soak for about 10 minutes.

2   Drain the chestnuts and create an aluminum foil pouch. Place the chestnuts in the pouch, sprinkle salt and pepper over them, drizzle the butter and olive oil on top, and add the thyme, cinnamon stick, and cloves to the pouch. Close the pouch, leaving an opening so that steam can escape.

3   Place the chestnuts in the oven and roast until tender, 40 to 45 minutes. Remove from the oven and serve warm.

PAIRS WELL WITH: HOLIDAY-THEMED BOARDS, FRUIT, PICKLED VEGETABLES

BAKED BRIE,
Two Ways

YIELD: 4 TO 6 SERVINGS / ACTIVE TIME: 10 MINUTES / TOTAL TIME: 25 MINUTES

INGREDIENTS

8 oz. Brie cheese

For the Savory Topping

¼ cup chopped roasted tomatoes

¼ cup chopped artichoke hearts

2 tablespoons pitted and chopped olives

1 tablespoon capers

Pinch of black pepper

For the Sweet Topping

¼ cup chopped pecans

¼ cup chopped dried apricots

⅓ cup Divina fig spread

¼ cup dried cherries

Pinch of cinnamon

1   Preheat the oven to 350°F. Combine the ingredients for your chosen topping in a mixing bowl.

2   Place the Brie in a ceramic dish and top it with the chosen topping.

3   Place the dish in the oven and bake for 15 minutes, until the cheese is gooey.

4   Remove from the oven and serve.

PAIRS WELL WITH: CROSTINI (SEE PAGE 51), CRUDITÉS, GAMAY & FRUITY REDS

CLASSIC
Fondue

YIELD: 6 SERVINGS / ACTIVE TIME: 10 MINUTES / TOTAL TIME: 20 MINUTES

INGREDIENTS

1 lb. Gruyère cheese, shredded

½ lb. Emmental cheese, shredded

½ lb. gouda cheese, shredded

2 tablespoons cornstarch

1 garlic clove, halved

1 cup white wine

1 tablespoon fresh lemon juice

Salt and pepper, to taste

Freshly grated nutmeg, to taste

1 Place the cheeses and cornstarch in a bowl and toss until the cheeses are evenly coated.

2 Rub the inside of a caquelon (fondue pot) with the garlic and place the pot over the flame to warm it up.

3 Place the wine and lemon juice in a saucepan and bring to a simmer over low heat. Add the cheese mixture and cook, stirring constantly, until the cheeses have melted and the mixture is smooth. Season with salt, pepper, and nutmeg, transfer the mixture to the fondue pot, and enjoy.

PAIRS WELL WITH: HOLIDAY-THEMED BOARDS, CRUSTY BREADS, ROASTED VEGETABLES

FONDUE FOLKLORE

A fun fondue tradition is to leave a thin layer of fondue at the bottom of the caquelon (fondue pot). By carefully controlling the heat, you can form this layer into a crust known as *La Religieuse*—"The Religious One." Lift it out and distribute it among your guests. You'll see why it is considered a delicacy.

CURRIED

Pistachios

YIELD: 4 SERVINGS / **ACTIVE TIME:** 10 MINUTES / **TOTAL TIME:** 30 MINUTES

INGREDIENTS

1 cup unshelled roasted pistachios

½ cup shelled roasted pistachios

½ teaspoon curry powder

1 tablespoon extra-virgin olive oil

½ teaspoon fine sea salt

1   Preheat the oven to 350°F. Place the pistachios in a mixing bowl, add the remaining ingredients, and toss until the nuts are coated.

2   Place the nuts on a baking sheet, place them in the oven, and roast until fragrant, about 12 minutes. Remove from the oven and let the pistachios cool before serving.

PAIRS WELL WITH: GOAT CHEESE, CRUDITÉS, POULTRY

SICILIAN
Bar Nuts

YIELD: 4 SERVINGS / ACTIVE TIME: 10 MINUTES / TOTAL TIME: 25 MINUTES

INGREDIENTS

¾ cup walnuts

¾ cup cashews

¾ cup pecan halves

2 tablespoons unsalted butter, melted

2 tablespoons chopped fresh rosemary

1 teaspoon cayenne pepper

1 tablespoon brown sugar

1 tablespoon flaky sea salt

1   Preheat the oven to 350°F. Place the nuts on a baking sheet, place them in the oven, and toast until fragrant, about 12 minutes. Remove from the oven and transfer the nuts to a mixing bowl.

2   Add the melted butter and toss until the nuts are evenly coated. Add the remaining ingredients, toss to coat, and serve.

PAIRS WELL WITH: SALTY CHEESES, CURED MEATS, FRUIT

SICILIAN BAR NUTS
SEE PAGE 259

GRANOLA

YIELD: 3 CUPS / **ACTIVE TIME:** 10 MINUTES / **TOTAL TIME:** 45 MINUTES

INGREDIENTS

2 cups rolled oats

¼ cup real maple syrup

1 cup pecan halves

2 teaspoons kosher salt

1 teaspoon cinnamon

⅔ cup dried cranberries

1 Preheat the oven to 350°F and line a baking sheet with a silpat mat. Place all the ingredients in a mixing bowl and toss to combine.

2 Spread the mixture on the baking sheet in an even layer. Place it in the oven and bake until browned and fragrant, about 20 minutes. Remove from the oven and let the granola cool completely before serving.

PAIRS WELL WITH: BAKED BRIE, HONEY, CURED MEATS

CURED

Egg Yolks

YIELD: 4 SERVINGS / **ACTIVE TIME:** 30 MINUTES / **TOTAL TIME:** 3 DAYS

INGREDIENTS

1½ cups kosher salt

½ cup sugar

4 egg yolks

1   Combine the salt and sugar in wide bowl. Using a spoon, create four small wells in the mixture, one for each yolk.

2   Carefully place each yolk into its own well. Spoon the mixture over the yolks until they are covered completely.

3   Cover the bowl with plastic wrap, place it in the refrigerator, and let the egg yolks cure for 3 days.

4   Remove the yolks from the mixture, rinse under cold water, and slice before serving.

PAIRS WELL WITH: SMOKED SEAFOOD, BREAKFAST & BRUNCH BOARDS, PICKLED VEGETABLES

BUTTERMILK
Waffles

YIELD: 4 SERVINGS / **ACTIVE TIME:** 20 MINUTES / **TOTAL TIME:** 30 MINUTES

INGREDIENTS

2 cups all-purpose flour

2 tablespoons sugar

2 teaspoons baking powder

½ teaspoon kosher salt

2 cups buttermilk

8 tablespoons unsalted butter, melted

2 eggs

1 Preheat a waffle iron. Place the flour, sugar, baking powder, and salt in a large bowl and whisk to combine.

2 Place the remaining ingredients in a separate mixing bowl, whisk to combine, and add the wet mixture to the dry mixture. Whisk until the mixture comes together as a smooth batter.

3 Pour the batter into the waffle iron and cook until browned and crispy.

PAIRS WELL WITH: BREAKFAST & BRUNCH BOARDS, FRIED FOODS

PAPAS

Rellenas

YIELD: 4 SERVINGS / ACTIVE TIME: 30 MINUTES / TOTAL TIME: 1 HOUR

INGREDIENTS

3 lbs. potatoes, peeled and chopped

1 garlic clove, minced

2 teaspoons kosher salt

1 teaspoon black pepper

1 tablespoon extra-virgin olive oil

1 small green bell pepper, stem and seeds removed, minced

1 yellow onion, minced

½ lb. ground beef

2 tablespoons tomato paste

¼ cup pitted and sliced green olives

¼ cup raisins

½ teaspoon paprika

Canola oil, as needed

2 eggs, lightly beaten

½ cup bread crumbs

1   Bring water to a boil in a large saucepan. Add the potatoes, cover the pan, and cook until the potatoes are fork-tender, about 20 minutes. Drain the potatoes, place them in a large bowl, and mash until smooth. Add the garlic and half of the salt and pepper and stir to incorporate.

2   Place the olive oil in a skillet and warm it over medium heat. When the oil starts to shimmer, add the bell pepper and onion and cook, stirring frequently, until the onion is translucent, about 3 minutes. Add the ground beef and cook, breaking it up with a fork, until it is browned, about 10 minutes. Stir in the tomato paste, olives, raisins, paprika, and the remaining salt and pepper and cook for 2 minutes. Transfer the mixture to a paper towel–lined baking sheet and let it drain.

3   Add canola oil to a Dutch oven until it is 2 inches deep and bring it to 375°F. Place the eggs and bread crumbs in two separate bowls. Place 2 tablespoons of the potato mixture in one hand, pat it down until it is flat, and then place a tablespoon of the ground beef mixture in the center. Shape the potato around the filling to create a ball and dredge the ball in the egg. Roll the ball in the bread crumbs until coated and place it on a parchment–lined baking sheet. Repeat until all of the potato mixture and ground beef mixture have been used up.

4   Working in batches, place the balls in the hot oil and deep-fry until golden brown, about 2 minutes. Remove with a slotted spoon and set them on a paper towel–lined plate to drain before enjoying.

PAIRS WELL WITH: PICKLED VEGETABLES, CURED MEATS, SALSAS & SPICY DIPS

CORNISH
Pasties

YIELD: 6 SERVINGS / ACTIVE TIME: 30 MINUTES / TOTAL TIME: 1 HOUR AND 15 MINUTES

INGREDIENTS

For the Dough

3 cups all-purpose flour, plus more as needed

¾ teaspoon kosher salt

½ cup lard or unsalted butter, cut into small pieces

1 large egg, beaten

¼ cup cold water, plus more as needed

2 teaspoons distilled white vinegar

For the Filling

¾ lb. skirt steak, cut into ½-inch cubes

¼ cup peeled and chopped parsnips

¼ cup peeled and chopped turnips

1 small onion, chopped

1 cup peeled and chopped potato

1 tablespoon chopped fresh thyme

2 tablespoons tomato paste

Salt and pepper, to taste

1 large egg, beaten

1 tablespoon water

1. To prepare the dough, place the flour and salt in a bowl, add the lard or butter, and use a pastry blender to work the mixture until it is coarse crumbs. Beat the egg, water, and vinegar together in a separate bowl and then drizzle this over the flour mixture. Use the pastry blender to work the mixture until it starts to hold together. Knead the dough with your hands, adding water in 1-teaspoon increments if it is too dry. Cut the dough into 6 pieces, cover them with plastic wrap, and chill in the refrigerator.

2. Preheat the oven to 400°F. To prepare the filling, place all the ingredients, except for the egg and water, in a bowl and stir to combine. Place the egg and water in a separate bowl and beat to combine.

3. Place the pieces of dough on a flour-dusted work surface, roll each one into an 8-inch circle, and place ½ cup of the filling in the center of each circle. Brush the edge of each circle with water, fold into a half-moon, and crimp the edge to seal, gently pressing down on the filling to remove as much air as possible. Place the sealed handpies on a parchment-lined baking sheet.

4. Brush the handpies with the egg wash and use a paring knife to make a small incision in the side of each one. Bake in the oven for 15 minutes, reduce the temperature to 350°F, and bake for another 25 minutes. Remove from the oven and let cool on a wire rack before serving.

PAIRS WELL WITH: BLUE CHEESES, DEVILED EGGS, PICKLED CABBAGE

PUNJABI
Samosas

YIELD: 16 SAMOSAS / **ACTIVE TIME:** 45 MINUTES / **TOTAL TIME:** 1 HOUR AND 30 MINUTES

1 To begin preparations for the wrappers, place the flour and salt in a mixing bowl and use your hands to combine. Add the oil and work the mixture with your hands until it is a coarse meal. Add the water and knead the mixture until a smooth, firm dough forms. If the dough is too dry, incorporate more water, adding 1 tablespoon at a time. Cover the bowl with a kitchen towel and set aside.

2 To begin preparations for the filling, place the potatoes in a saucepan and cover with water. Bring the water to a boil and cook until fork-tender, about 20 minutes. Transfer to a bowl, mash until smooth, and set aside.

3 Place the olive oil in a skillet and warm over medium heat. Add the crushed seeds and toast until fragrant, about 2 minutes, shaking the pan frequently. Add the ginger, garlic, and jalapeño, stir-fry for 2 minutes, and then add the chili powder, turmeric, amchoor powder, and garam masala. Cook for another minute before adding the mashed potatoes. Stir to combine, season with salt, and taste the mixture. Adjust the seasoning as necessary, transfer the mixture to a bowl, and let it cool completely.

4 Divide the dough for the wrappers into eight pieces and roll each one out into a 6-inch circle on a flour-dusted work surface. Cut the circles in half and brush the flat edge of each piece with water. Fold one corner of the flat edge toward the other to make a cone and pinch to seal. Fill each cone one-third of the way with the filling, brush the opening with water, and pinch to seal. Place the sealed samosas on a parchment-lined baking sheet.

5 Add canola oil to a Dutch oven until it is 2 inches deep and warm to 325°F over medium heat. Working in batches, add the filled samosas to the hot oil and fry, turning them as they cook, until they are golden brown, about 5 minutes. Transfer the cooked samosas to a paper towel–lined plate and serve once they have all been cooked.

PAIRS WELL WITH: CREAMY DIPS, SPICED NUTS, FRUIT

INGREDIENTS

For the Wrappers

2 cups maida flour, plus more as needed

¼ teaspoon kosher salt

2 tablespoons extra-virgin olive oil

½ cup water, plus more as needed

For the Filling

2 russet potatoes, peeled and chopped

2 tablespoons extra-virgin olive oil

1 teaspoon coriander seeds, crushed

½ teaspoon fennel seeds, crushed

Pinch of fenugreek seeds, crushed

1-inch piece of fresh ginger, peeled and grated

1 garlic clove, grated

1 teaspoon minced jalapeño chile pepper

2 teaspoons chili powder

¾ teaspoon turmeric

1 tablespoon amchoor powder

½ teaspoon garam masala

Salt, to taste

Canola oil, as needed

CHEESY
Poofs

YIELD: 4 SERVINGS / ACTIVE TIME: 15 MINUTES / TOTAL TIME: 35 MINUTES

INGREDIENTS

Canola oil, as needed

2 cups sweet potato puree

1 egg

½ cup white flour

½ teaspoon baking powder

¼ cup grated Asiago cheese

¼ cup grated Parmesan cheese

⅓ cup shredded mozzarella cheese

1   Add canola oil to a Dutch oven until it is 3 inches deep and warm to 350°F over medium heat. Place the sweet potato puree and egg in a mixing bowl. Add the flour and baking powder and stir until the mixture is smooth.

2   Add the cheeses one at a time and fold to incorporate. Form tablespoons of the mixture into balls and gently slip them into the oil. Turn the balls as they cook until they are golden brown. Remove and drain on a paper towel–lined plate before serving.

PAIRS WELL WITH: SPICY DIPS, CURED MEATS, CRUDITÉS

SMOKY & SPICY
Almonds

YIELD: 2 CUPS / **ACTIVE TIME:** 10 MINUTES / **TOTAL TIME:** 45 MINUTES

INGREDIENTS

4 tablespoons unsalted butter, melted

4 teaspoons Worcestershire sauce

1 teaspoon cumin

2 teaspoons chili powder

1 teaspoon garlic powder

½ teaspoon onion powder

1 teaspoon cayenne pepper

1 teaspoon kosher salt

2 cups whole almonds

1   Preheat the oven to 350°F and line a baking sheet with parchment paper. Place all the ingredients, except for the almonds, in a mixing bowl and stir until combined.

2   Add the almonds and toss to coat.

3   Transfer the almonds to the baking sheet, place it in the oven, and roast for about 15 minutes, until the almonds are fragrant and slightly darker. Turn the almonds occasionally as they roast.

4   Remove from the oven and let the almonds cool before serving.

PAIRS WELL WITH: FRUIT, CURED MEATS, BLUE CHEESES

KACHORI

YIELD: 20 DUMPLINGS / ACTIVE TIME: 45 MINUTES / TOTAL TIME: 1 HOUR

INGREDIENTS

1 cup all-purpose flour, plus more as needed

½ teaspoon kosher salt

1 tablespoon avocado oil, plus more as needed

2 tablespoons semolina flour

Juice of 1 lemon

⅓ to ½ cup water

1 tablespoon extra-virgin olive oil

½ teaspoon asafetida

2 cups fresh green peas or defrosted frozen peas

1 large jalapeño chile pepper, stems and seeds removed, minced

2 tablespoons grated ginger

1 tablespoon garam masala

1 tablespoon coarsely ground fennel seeds

1 teaspoon fine sea salt

½ teaspoon sugar

1 Place the all-purpose flour, kosher salt, avocado oil, semolina flour, and half of the lemon juice in a large bowl. Gradually add ⅓ cup of water, stirring with a wooden spoon until the mixture comes together as a dough. Knead the dough until it is smooth, about 3 to 5 minutes. If the dough feels too dry, add water 1 tablespoon at a time until the dough is stiff and not too sticky. Cover the dough with a towel and set aside.

2 Place the olive oil in a large skillet and warm it over medium heat. Add the asafetida and cook until it sizzles, 2 to 4 minutes. Add the peas and ¼ cup water, cover the pan, and cook until the peas are tender and the water has evaporated, about 5 minutes.

3 Add the jalapeño, ginger, garam masala, fennel seeds, sea salt, sugar, and remaining lemon juice and stir to combine. Cook the mixture until the jalapeño is tender, 10 to 15 minutes. Remove the pan from heat, coarsely mash the mixture with a potato masher, and let it cool for 15 minutes.

4 Add avocado oil to a Dutch oven until it is 2 inches deep and warm it to 350°F.

5 Place the dough on a flour-dusted work surface. Roll out the dough until it is an approximately ¹⁄₁₆-inch-thick circle. Cut the dough into 2-inch circles and roll them out until they are about 4 inches. Place 1 tablespoon of the cooled filling in the center of each circle, bring the edges of the dough toward the center, and fold them over the filling to form little baskets. Crimp the edges of the dough to seal.

6 Working in batches, gently slip the dumplings into the oil and fry until they are golden brown, 4 to 5 minutes, turning them as necessary. Transfer the cooked dumplings to a paper towel–lined plate to drain before enjoying.

PAIRS WELL WITH: CREAMY DIPS, CRUDITÉS, POULTRY

LEMON

Ricotta

YIELD: 2 CUPS / **ACTIVE TIME:** 10 MINUTES / **TOTAL TIME:** 3 HOURS

INGREDIENTS

4 cups whole milk

Juice of 2 lemons

1 tablespoon kosher salt

1   Place the milk in a saucepan and warm it over medium heat until it is just about to come to a boil (about 190°F). Remove the pan from heat, add the lemon juice, and stir for 1 minute. Cover the pan and let the mixture stand for 15 minutes. This will allow the curds to separate.

2   Ladle the curds into cheesecloth, tie it closed with kitchen twine, and let it drain at room temperature until almost all the liquid has been drained, about 2½ hours. Stir the salt into the ricotta and enjoy.

PAIRS WELL WITH: CRUSTY BREADS, MEATBALLS, FRUIT

PARMESAN
Crisps

YIELD: 24 CRISPS / ACTIVE TIME: 10 MINUTES / TOTAL TIME: 25 MINUTES

INGREDIENTS

2 cups freshly grated Parmesan cheese

2 tablespoons Everything Bagel Seasoning (see page 90)

2 tablespoons all-purpose flour

1 Preheat the oven to 350°F and line a baking sheet with a silpat mat. Place all the ingredients in a food processor and blitz until combined.

2 Using a 2-inch ring mold, shape the mixture into rounds on the baking sheet. You want the rounds to be about ¼ inch thick.

3 Place the pan in the oven and bake until the rounds are brown and crispy, about 7 minutes. Remove from the oven and let cool before enjoying.

PAIRS WELL WITH: CRUDITÉS, CURED MEATS, SHARP-FLAVORED CHEESES

PARMESAN
Spheres

YIELD: 2 SERVINGS / ACTIVE TIME: 45 MINUTES / TOTAL TIME: 1 HOUR AND 45 MINUTES

INGREDIENTS

4 cups freshly grated Parmesan cheese

1 cup egg whites

4 cups canola oil

1. Line a baking sheet with parchment paper. Place the cheese and egg whites in a food processor and blitz until pureed. Scoop ¼-cup portions of the puree onto the baking sheet and place it in the freezer for 45 minutes.

2. Add the canola oil to a Dutch oven and warm it to 350°F over medium heat. Working in batches, add the spheres to the oil and fry, turning occasionally, until they are golden brown, about 4 minutes. Transfer the cooked spheres to a paper towel–lined plate to drain and serve once they have all been cooked.

PAIRS WELL WITH: GARLICKY DIPS, COLD CUTS

GRILLED

Halloumi

YIELD: 4 SERVINGS / ACTIVE TIME: 5 MINUTES / TOTAL TIME: 20 MINUTES

INGREDIENTS

8 oz. halloumi cheese

Extra-virgin olive oil, to taste

1 Preheat a gas or charcoal grill to 350°F. Cut the halloumi into pieces that are approximately ½ inch wide.

2 Drizzle olive oil over the cheese and place it on the grill. Grill until the cheese is warm and has grill marks on both sides, about 6 minutes. Remove from the grill and serve immediately.

PAIRS WELL WITH: FLATBREADS, OLIVES, MEDITERRANEAN-THEMED BOARDS

MARINATED
Feta

YIELD: 4 SERVINGS / ACTIVE TIME: 5 MINUTES / TOTAL TIME: 2 HOURS AND 5 MINUTES

INGREDIENTS

8 oz. feta cheese

1 sprig of fresh basil

¾ cup extra-virgin olive oil

½ cup white wine vinegar

2 tablespoons black pepper

1 teaspoon kosher salt

¾ teaspoon red pepper flakes

1   Cut the feta into bite-size chunks and place them in a mason jar.

2   Combine the remaining ingredients in a mixing bowl and then pour the marinade over the feta. Let the cheese marinate for at least 2 hours before serving.

PAIRS WELL WITH: CRUDITÉS, CURED MEATS, NUTS

MARINATED
Mozzarella

YIELD: 4 SERVINGS / **ACTIVE TIME:** 5 MINUTES / **TOTAL TIME:** 5 MINUTES

INGREDIENTS

1 (7 oz.) container of miniature balls of mozzarella cheese

Pesto (see page 154)

1　Place the mozzarella and Pesto in a mixing bowl, toss until the cheese is coated, and serve immediately.

PAIRS WELL WITH: SPICY CURED MEATS, FLATBREADS, SUMMER VEGETABLES

BAKED

Camembert

YIELD: 4 SERVINGS / ACTIVE TIME: 5 MINUTES / TOTAL TIME: 25 MINUTES

INGREDIENTS

8 oz. Camembert cheese

1 cup Granola (see page 262)

½ cup real maple syrup

1 Preheat the oven to 350°F. Place the Camembert in a small cast-iron skillet or a ceramic dish. Sprinkle the granola over the cheese and drizzle the maple syrup on top.

2 Place in the oven and bake until the cheese is gooey, about 15 minutes. Remove from the oven and serve immediately.

PAIRS WELL WITH: PROSCIUTTO, NUTS, DARK BREADS

GOAT CHEESE
with Herbs

YIELD: 4 SERVINGS / ACTIVE TIME: 10 MINUTES / TOTAL TIME: 1 HOUR AND 10 MINUTES

INGREDIENTS

8 oz. goat cheese

2 tablespoons chopped fresh tarragon

2 tablespoons chopped fresh chives

2 tablespoons chopped fresh thyme

1 cup extra-virgin olive oil

2 garlic cloves, chopped

1 teaspoon kosher salt

1   Slice the goat cheese into rounds. Gently roll the rounds in the herbs and gently press down so that the herbs adhere to the cheese.

2   Layer the rounds in glass jars. Pour the olive oil over them until they are covered. Add the garlic and salt and let the mixture sit for an hour before serving.

PAIRS WELL WITH: CROSTINI (SEE PAGE 51), CRUDITÉS, SUMMER-THEMED BOARDS

SOUTHERN
Deviled Eggs

YIELD: 6 EGGS / ACTIVE TIME: 15 MINUTES / TOTAL TIME: 30 MINUTES

INGREDIENTS

6 hard-boiled eggs

2 tablespoons yellow mustard

2 tablespoons mayonnaise

2 teaspoons whole-grain mustard

2 cornichons, diced

2 teaspoons diced pimiento pepper

Salt and pepper, to taste

Fresh parsley, chopped, for garnish

Fresh dill, chopped, for garnish

1 slice of Spam, cut into triangles and fried, for garnish (optional)

1 Cut the eggs in half, remove the yolks, and place them in a small bowl. Add all the ingredients, except for the garnishes, and stir until thoroughly combined.

2 Spoon the yolk mixture into the cavities in the egg whites. Garnish with parsley, dill, and, if desired, the Spam.

PAIRS WELL WITH: CURED MEATS, PICKLED VEGETABLES

RETURN TO THE GARDEN

Cheese and cured meat get all the attention when it comes to the charcuterie board, but fruits and vegetables, with their ability to highlight the best of each season as well as what's available locally, are just as worthy of celebration. This elevation is due to their ability to star in a supporting role, pairing beautifully with numerous foods, and adding subtle, unique notes to your boards.

CAPONATA

YIELD: 6 SERVINGS / **ACTIVE TIME:** 1 HOUR / **TOTAL TIME:** 2 HOURS

INGREDIENTS

1 large eggplant (about 1½ lbs.)

2 tablespoons extra-virgin olive oil

1 onion, chopped

2 celery stalks, peeled and chopped

3 large garlic cloves, minced

2 red bell peppers, stems and seeds removed, chopped

Salt and pepper, to taste

1 lb. ripe Roma tomatoes, peeled, seeds removed, and finely chopped; or 1 (14 oz.) can of crushed tomatoes, with their liquid

2 tablespoons sugar, plus a pinch

3 generous tablespoons capers, rinsed and drained

3 tablespoons chopped green olives

3 tablespoons red wine vinegar

1 Preheat the oven to 425°F. Place the eggplant on a baking sheet, place it in the oven, and roast until it has collapsed and is starting to char, about 25 minutes. Remove from the oven and let the eggplant cool. When cool enough to handle, roughly chop the eggplant.

2 Place 1 tablespoon of the oil in a large skillet and warm it over medium heat. When the oil starts to shimmer, add the onion and celery and cook, stirring, until the onion starts to soften, about 5 minutes. Stir in the garlic, cook for 1 minute, and then add the peppers. Season with salt and cook, stirring frequently, until the peppers are tender, about 8 minutes.

3 Add the remaining olive oil and the eggplant and cook, stirring occasionally, until the eggplant begins to fall apart and the other vegetables are tender. Stir in the tomatoes and the pinch of sugar, season the mixture with salt, and cook, stirring frequently, until the tomatoes start to collapse and smell fragrant, about 7 minutes.

4 Stir in the capers, olives, remaining sugar, and vinegar. Reduce the heat to medium-low and cook, stirring often, until the mixture is quite thick, sweet, and fragrant, 20 to 30 minutes. Taste, season with salt and pepper, and remove the pan from heat. Let the caponata cool to room temperature before serving. If time allows, chill in the refrigerator overnight and let it return to room temperature before serving.

PAIRS WELL WITH: ITALIAN-THEMED BOARDS, CROSTINI (SEE PAGE 51), MILD & CREAMY CHEESES

ZUCCHINI
Sott'olio

YIELD: 4 SERVINGS / **ACTIVE TIME:** 15 MINUTES / **TOTAL TIME:** 24 HOURS

INGREDIENTS

¼ cup kosher salt, plus more as needed

2 zucchini, trimmed and sliced

4 anchovy fillets in olive oil, rinsed and deboned

1 garlic clove

Extra-virgin olive oil, as needed

1   Bring 8 cups of water to a boil in a medium saucepan. Add the salt and the zucchini and cook until the zucchini is just tender, about 4 minutes. Drain and let the zucchini cool.

2   Taste the zucchini. It should taste too salty, which is what you want in this particular preparation. If not, season with salt until it tastes too salty.

3   Place the zucchini in a jar, add the anchovies and garlic, and cover the mixture with olive oil. Place the mixture in the refrigerator and let it sit overnight before serving.

PAIRS WELL WITH: SUMMER-THEMED BOARDS, NUTTY & SHARP CHEESES, SMOKED MEATS

ROASTED
Grapes

YIELD: 8 SERVINGS / ACTIVE TIME: 10 MINUTES / TOTAL TIME: 1 HOUR AND 30 MINUTES

INGREDIENTS

1½ to 2 lbs. red seedless grapes, rinsed and patted dry

Extra-virgin olive oil, as needed

Salt, to taste

1   Preheat the oven to 350°F. Place the grapes in a mixing bowl, drizzle olive oil generously over them, and toss to coat. Place the grapes on a baking sheet, season with salt, and place in the oven. Roast until most of the grapes have collapsed and are slightly charred, about 30 minutes.

2   Remove from the oven and let cool completely before serving—the longer you let the grapes sit, the more concentrated their flavor will become.

PAIRS WELL WITH: SHARP CHEESES, SUMMER-THEMED BOARDS, SPICED NUTS

PEPERONATA

YIELD: 6 SERVINGS / **ACTIVE TIME:** 30 MINUTES / **TOTAL TIME:** 2 HOURS

INGREDIENTS

½ cup extra-virgin olive oil

4 large garlic cloves, sliced thin

1 red onion, halved and sliced

2 teaspoons kosher salt, plus more to taste

Black pepper, to taste

4 red bell peppers, stems and seeds removed, sliced thin

1 tablespoon sherry vinegar

1 tablespoon dried oregano

½ cup pitted black olives

Caper berries, drained, for garnish (optional)

1 Place a rack in the middle position in the oven and preheat the oven to 400°F. Place the olive oil in a large skillet and warm it over medium-high heat. When the oil starts to shimmer, add the garlic and onion and cook, stirring frequently, until they begin to soften, about 2 minutes.

2 Season with salt and pepper, add the bell peppers, and cook, stirring occasionally, until the peppers begin to soften, about 10 minutes.

3 Stir in the sherry vinegar and oregano and cook for another 2 minutes. Transfer the mixture to a large baking dish and use a wooden spoon to make sure it is distributed evenly.

4 Top with the olives, place the dish in the oven, and bake until the edges of the peperonata start to char, 1 to 1½ hours. Remove from the oven, top the peperonata with the caper berries (if desired), and serve.

PAIRS WELL WITH: CROSTINI (SEE PAGE 51), MILD CHEESES, CURED MEATS

CAPRESE
Salad

YIELD: 4 SERVINGS / ACTIVE TIME: 15 MINUTES / TOTAL TIME: 15 MINUTES

INGREDIENTS

1 lb. heirloom tomatoes, sliced (in season is a must)

Salt and pepper, to taste

1 lb. fresh mozzarella cheese, sliced

¼ cup Pesto (see page 154)

Quality extra-virgin olive oil, to taste

1 Season the tomatoes with salt and pepper. While alternating, arrange them and the slices of mozzarella on a platter.

2 Drizzle the Pesto and olive oil over the tomatoes and mozzarella and serve.

PAIRS WELL WITH: SUMMER-THEMED BOARDS, CRUSTY BREADS, HERB-BASED CONDIMENTS

ROASTED *Garlic*

YIELD: 6 SERVINGS / **ACTIVE TIME:** 15 MINUTES / **TOTAL TIME:** 45 MINUTES

INGREDIENTS

6 heads of garlic

Extra-virgin olive oil, as needed

Salt, to taste

1 Preheat the oven to 375°F. Cut the top off each head of garlic and place the heads of garlic, cut side up, in a baking dish that is small enough for them to fit snugly. Add about ¼ inch of water to the dish, drizzle olive oil over the garlic, and sprinkle with salt.

2 Cover the dish with aluminum foil, place it in the oven, and roast for 20 minutes. Lift the foil and test to see if the garlic is tender and browned. If not, re-cover the dish, add water if it has evaporated, and roast for another 10 minutes. Remove from the oven and serve.

PAIRS WELL WITH: CRUSTY BREADS, NUTS, OLIVES

FRIED
Brussels Sprouts

YIELD: 4 SERVINGS / **ACTIVE TIME:** 30 MINUTES / **TOTAL TIME:** 30 MINUTES

INGREDIENTS

Canola oil, as needed

3 cups Brussels sprouts, trimmed and halved

Salt and pepper, to taste

1 Add canola oil to a Dutch oven until it is about 2 inches deep and warm it to 350°F over medium heat.

2 Working in batches so as not to crowd the pot, gently slip the Brussels sprouts into the oil and fry until crispy and golden brown, 2 to 3 minutes. Transfer to a paper towel–lined plate and let the Brussels sprouts drain.

3 Place the Brussels sprouts in a bowl, season with salt and pepper, transfer to a serving dish, and enjoy.

PAIRS WELL WITH: SPICY CONDIMENTS, CREAMY CHEESES, NUTS

TOMATO
Aguachile

YIELD: 4 SERVINGS / ACTIVE TIME: 20 MINUTES / TOTAL TIME: 12 HOURS

INGREDIENTS

2 lbs. Roma tomatoes

1 guajillo chile pepper, stemmed and seeded

4 dried chiles de arbol

Salt, to taste

1 cup fresh lime juice

1 lb. cherry tomatoes, halved

1 cup peeled and diced cucumber

Extra-virgin olive oil, to taste

2 cups shredded queso fresco

1 small red onion, julienned

1 serrano chile pepper, stems and seeds removed, sliced very thin

1 small bunch of fresh cilantro

1　Place the Roma tomatoes and dried chiles in a blender and pulse until the mixture is a coarse puree. Line a fine-mesh sieve or colander with cheesecloth, place it over a bowl, and pour the puree into the cheesecloth. Let the "tomato water" drip through for a minimum of 8 hours.

2　Season the tomato water with salt, stir in the lime juice, and set it aside. The pulp can be reserved, dehydrated, and turned into a flavorful seasoning powder.

3　In a mixing bowl, combine the cherry tomatoes, cucumber, and tomato water and drizzle a bit of olive oil over the mixture.

4　Transfer the mixture to a shallow bowl and top with the queso fresco, red onion, serrano pepper, and cilantro. Sprinkle a flaky sea salt over the dish, preferably Maldon, and enjoy.

PAIRS WELL WITH: SPICY FOODS, SUMMER-THEMED BOARDS, TORTILLA CHIPS

SPANISH
Tortilla

YIELD: 6 SERVINGS / **ACTIVE TIME:** 30 MINUTES / **TOTAL TIME:** 2 HOURS

INGREDIENTS

5 large russet potatoes, peeled and sliced thin

1 Spanish onion, sliced

½ cup canola oil, plus more as needed

½ cup olive oil

10 eggs, at room temperature

Large pinch of kosher salt

1   Place the potatoes, onion, canola oil, and olive oil in a 12-inch cast-iron skillet. The potatoes should be submerged. If not, add more canola oil as needed. Bring to a gentle simmer over low heat and cook until the potatoes are tender, about 30 minutes. Remove from heat and let cool slightly.

2   Use a slotted spoon to remove the potatoes and onion from the oil. Reserve the oil. Place the eggs and salt in a large bowl and whisk to combine. Add the potatoes and onion to the eggs.

3   Warm the skillet over high heat. Add ¼ cup of the reserved oil and swirl to coat the bottom and sides of the pan. Pour the egg-and-potato mixture into the pan and stir vigorously to ensure that the mixture does not stick to the sides. Cook for 1 minute and remove from heat. Place the pan over low heat, cover, and cook for 3 minutes.

4   Carefully invert the tortilla onto a large plate. Return it to the skillet, cook for 3 minutes, and then invert it onto the plate. Return it to the skillet and cook for another 3 minutes. Remove the tortilla from the pan and let it rest at room temperature for 1 hour before serving.

PAIRS WELL WITH: CURED MEATS, BRUNCH BOARDS, OLIVES

DUDHI
Kofta

YIELD: 6 SERVINGS / **ACTIVE TIME:** 30 MINUTES / **TOTAL TIME:** 1 HOUR AND 30 MINUTES

INGREDIENTS

2 lbs. zucchini, trimmed and grated

2 teaspoons kosher salt

1 small red onion, chopped

¼ cup raw cashews

2 garlic cloves, minced

1-inch piece of fresh ginger, peeled and grated

4 bird's eye chile peppers, stems and seeds removed, and minced

½ cup chickpea flour

2 tablespoons chopped fresh cilantro

4 cups canola oil

1 Place the grated zucchini in a bowl, add the salt, and stir to combine. Let stand for 20 minutes.

2 Place the onion, cashews, garlic, ginger, and chiles in a food processor and blitz until the mixture becomes a chunky paste.

3 Place the zucchini in a kitchen towel and wring it to remove as much liquid as possible. Place the zucchini in a mixing bowl and add the onion-and-cashew paste. Stir to combine, add the chickpea flour and cilantro, and fold to incorporate. The dough should be slightly wet.

4 Place the canola oil in a Dutch oven and heat it to 300°F. As the oil warms, form tablespoons of the dough into balls and place them on a parchment-lined baking sheet. When the oil is ready, place the dumplings in the oil and fry until golden brown, about 5 minutes. Work in batches if necessary. Transfer the cooked dumplings to a paper towel–lined plate to drain before serving.

PAIRS WELL WITH: SUMMER-THEMED & VEGETARIAN BOARDS, MILD CHEESES, SPICY DIPS

BREAD & BUTTER
Pickles

YIELD: ½ CUP / **ACTIVE TIME:** 5 MINUTES / **TOTAL TIME:** 6 HOURS

INGREDIENTS

2 Persian cucumbers, sliced thin

1 small onion, sliced thin

2 jalapeño chile peppers, sliced thin

4 sprigs of fresh dill

2 tablespoons coriander seeds

2 tablespoons mustard seeds

2 teaspoons celery salt

2 cups distilled white vinegar

1 cup sugar

2 tablespoons kosher salt

1 Place the cucumbers, onion, jalapeños, dill, coriander seeds, mustard seeds, and celery salt in a 1-quart mason jar.

2 Place the vinegar, sugar, and salt in a medium saucepan and bring it to a boil, stirring to dissolve the sugar and salt. Carefully pour the brine into jar, filling all the way to the top. If you want to can these pickles, see the sidebar on the opposite page. If you do not want to can the pickles, let the mixture cool completely before sealing and storing in the refrigerator, where they will keep for up to 1 week.

PAIRS WELL WITH: SEAFOOD, COLD CUTS, NUTTY CHEESES

CANNING 101

Bring a pot of water to a boil. Place your mason jars in the water for 15 to 20 minutes to sterilize them. Do not boil the mason jar lids, as this can prevent them from creating a proper seal when the time comes.

Bring water to a boil in a large canning pot. Fill the sterilized mason jars with whatever you are canning. Place the lids on the jars and secure the bands tightly. Place the jars in the boiling water for 40 minutes. Use a pair of canning tongs to remove the jars from the boiling water and let them cool. As they are cooling, you should hear the classic "ping and pop" sound of the lids creating a seal.

After 6 hours, check the lids. There should be no give in them, and they should be suctioned onto the jars. Discard any lids and food that did not seal properly.

PURPLE
Potato Chips

YIELD: 6 SERVINGS / **ACTIVE TIME:** 5 MINUTES / **TOTAL TIME:** 20 MINUTES

INGREDIENTS

3 large purple potatoes, sliced thin

¼ cup extra-virgin olive oil

2 teaspoons fine sea salt

1   Preheat the oven to 400°F.

2   Place the potatoes, olive oil, and salt in a bowl and toss until the potatoes are evenly coated. Place the potatoes on a baking sheet in a single layer. Bake for 12 to 15 minutes, until crispy.

3   Remove from the oven and serve warm or store in an airtight container, where they will keep for up to 1 week.

PAIRS WELL WITH: SEAFOOD, FOIE GRAS, CURED MEATS

FRIED

Squash Blossoms

YIELD: 4 SERVINGS / ACTIVE TIME: 20 MINUTES / TOTAL TIME: 50 MINUTES

INGREDIENTS

10 squash blossoms, stamens removed

1 bunch of fresh spearmint

2 cups shredded queso fresco

Zest and juice of 1 lemon

Salt, to taste

1 cup all-purpose flour

1 teaspoon baking powder

2 egg yolks

1 cup seltzer water

2 cups canola oil

1 Place the squash blossoms on a paper towel–lined baking sheet.

2 Finely chop the spearmint and combine it with the queso fresco. Add the lemon zest and juice, season the mixture with the salt, and stir to combine.

3 Stuff the squash blossoms with the mixture, taking care not to tear the flowers.

4 In a small bowl, combine the flour, baking powder, egg yolks, and seltzer water and work the mixture with a whisk until it is a smooth batter. Let the batter rest for 20 minutes.

5 Place the canola oil in a deep skillet and warm to 350°F over medium heat.

6 Fold the tips of the squash blossoms closed and dip them into the batter. Gently slip them into the oil and fry until crispy and golden brown all over, about 2 minutes, making sure you only turn the squash blossoms once.

7 Drain the fried squash blossoms on the baking sheet. Season them lightly with salt and enjoy.

PAIRS WELL WITH: SMOKED MEATS, HONEYCOMB, SPICED NUTS

VEGETARIAN
Taquitos

YIELD: 4 SERVINGS / ACTIVE TIME: 20 MINUTES / TOTAL TIME: 35 MINUTES

INGREDIENTS

2 poblano chile peppers

2 cups ricotta cheese

Salt, to taste

8 corn tortillas

¼ cup extra-virgin olive oil

1 Roast the poblano chiles over an open flame, on the grill, or in the oven until charred all over. Place the poblanos in a bowl, cover it with plastic wrap, and let them steam for 10 minutes. When cool enough to handle, remove the skins, seeds, and stems from the poblanos and slice the remaining flesh thin.

2 Stir the poblanos into the ricotta, season with salt, and set the mixture aside.

3 Place the tortillas in a dry skillet and warm for 1 minute on each side. Fill the tortillas with the cheese-and-poblano mixture and roll them up tight.

4 Place the oil in a skillet and warm it over medium heat. Place the tortillas in the pan, seam side down, and cook for 1 minute before turning them over. Cook the taquitos until brown on all sides and place on a paper towel–lined plate to drain before enjoying.

PAIRS WELL WITH: SPICY & CREAMY DIPS, CURED MEATS, CRUDITÉS

PICKLED
Pineapple

YIELD: 4 SERVINGS / **ACTIVE TIME:** 40 MINUTES / **TOTAL TIME:** 2 DAYS

INGREDIENTS

2 star anise pods

½ cinnamon stick

2 dried chiles de arbol

2¼ cups apple cider vinegar

7 tablespoons white vinegar

3 tablespoons sugar

Salt, to taste

1 pineapple, peeled, cored, and sliced

1   Preheat a gas or charcoal grill to medium heat (400°F).

2   Place the star anise, cinnamon stick, and chiles in a saucepan and toast until they are fragrant, about 2 minutes, shaking the pan frequently. Add the vinegars and sugar, generously season with salt, and bring to a boil, stirring to dissolve the sugar.

3   Pour the brine into a sterilized mason jar.

4   Place the pineapple on the grill and grill until charred on both sides, about 8 minutes. Add the pineapple to the brine while it is still warm and let the mixture cool to room temperature. Cover and refrigerate for 2 days before using.

PAIRS WELL WITH: CURED MEATS, SUMMER-THEMED BOARDS, SPICY CONDIMENTS

PICKLED

Rhubarb

YIELD: 4 SERVINGS / ACTIVE TIME: 10 MINUTES / TOTAL TIME: 2 HOURS

INGREDIENTS

½ cup red wine

½ cup red wine vinegar

½ cup sugar

2 sprigs of fresh mint

Zest and juice of 1 orange

1 cup finely diced rhubarb

1 Place the red wine, red wine vinegar, and sugar in a medium saucepan and bring it to a boil.

2 Stir in the remaining ingredients and remove the pan from heat. Pour the mixture into a sterilized mason jar and let it cool to room temperature.

3 If canning, see page 325. If not, chill in the refrigerator for 1 hour before serving.

PAIRS WELL WITH: SPRING-THEMED BOARDS, DARK BREADS, NUTTY CHEESES

STRAWBERRY
Chips

YIELD: 4 SERVINGS / ACTIVE TIME: 15 MINUTES / TOTAL TIME: 3 HOURS

INGREDIENTS

½ cup water

½ cup sugar

1 teaspoon pure vanilla extract

1 cup hulled and thinly sliced strawberries

1 Place the water and sugar in a small saucepan and bring to a boil, stirring to dissolve the sugar. Stir in the vanilla, remove the pan from heat, and let the syrup cool.

2 Dip the strawberries in the syrup and place them on a parchment-lined baking sheet. Place in a food dehydrator set at 140°F and dehydrate for 1 hour.

3 Turn the strawberries over and dehydrate for another 1½ hours.

4 Remove from the dehydrator and either serve immediately or store in an airtight container.

PAIRS WELL WITH: PÂTÉ, TOAST POINTS (SEE PAGE 52), SHARP CHEESES

FALAFEL

YIELD: 4 SERVINGS / **ACTIVE TIME:** 30 MINUTES / **TOTAL TIME**: 2 HOURS

INGREDIENTS

1 (14 oz.) can of chickpeas, drained and rinsed

½ red onion, chopped

1 cup fresh parsley, chopped

1 cup fresh cilantro, chopped

3 bunches of scallions, trimmed and chopped

1 jalapeño chile pepper, stems and seeds removed, and chopped

3 garlic cloves

1 teaspoon cumin

1 teaspoon kosher salt, plus more to taste

½ teaspoon cardamom

¼ teaspoon black pepper

2 tablespoons chickpea flour

½ teaspoon baking soda

4 cups canola oil

1   Line a baking sheet with parchment paper. Place all of the ingredients, except for the canola oil, in a food processor and blitz until pureed. Scoop ¼-cup portions of the puree onto the baking sheet and place it in the refrigerator for 1 hour.

2   Add the canola oil to a Dutch oven and warm it to 350°F over medium heat. Working in batches, add the falafel to the oil and fry, turning occasionally, until they are golden brown, about 6 minutes. Transfer the cooked falafel to a paper towel–lined plate to drain. Serve once all of the falafel have been cooked.

PAIRS WELL WITH: VEGETARIAN BOARDS, CREAMY DIPS, OLIVES

FALAFEL
SEE PAGE 337

ROASTED
Tomatoes

YIELD: 4 SERVINGS / ACTIVE TIME: 5 MINUTES / TOTAL TIME: 30 MINUTES

INGREDIENTS

12 grape tomatoes, on the vine

Extra-virgin olive oil, to taste

Salt and pepper, to taste

1   Preheat the oven to 350°F. Place the tomatoes on a baking sheet, drizzle olive oil over them, and season with salt and pepper.

2   Place the tomatoes in the oven and roast until they are blistered and starting to collapse, about 10 minutes. Remove from the oven and let the tomatoes cool briefly before serving.

PAIRS WELL WITH: SUMMER-THEMED BOARDS, FLATBREADS, SPICY FOODS

PICKLED
Avocado

YIELD: 4 SERVINGS / ACTIVE TIME: 15 MINUTES / TOTAL TIME: 4 HOURS AND 30 MINUTES

INGREDIENTS

1 cup white wine vinegar

1 cup water

⅓ cup sugar

1 tablespoon kosher salt

1 teaspoon red pepper flakes

Flesh of 2 firm avocados

1 garlic clove, smashed

5 sprigs of fresh cilantro

1   Place the vinegar, water, sugar, salt, and red pepper flakes in a medium saucepan and bring to a boil, stirring to dissolve the sugar. Remove the pan from heat and let the brine cool completely.

2   Cut the avocados into wedges and place them in a sterilized mason jar along with the garlic and cilantro. Pour the cooled brine into the jar. If canning, see page 325. If not, place the jar in the refrigerator and let the avocado pickle for at least 4 hours before serving.

PAIRS WELL WITH: SEAFOOD, PICKLED VEGETABLES, BUTTERY CRACKERS

CHARRED
Escabeche

YIELD: 6 SERVINGS / ACTIVE TIME: 30 MINUTES / TOTAL TIME: 24 HOURS

INGREDIENTS

3½ tablespoons water

2⅓ tablespoons apple cider vinegar

¼ cup white vinegar

1 tablespoon sugar

1 tablespoon kosher salt

2 sprigs of fresh thyme

2 garlic cloves

2 bay leaves

5 oz. jalapeño chile peppers, halved

1⅓ lbs. carrots, peeled and sliced on a bias

1 Place the water, vinegars, sugar, and salt in a saucepan and bring to a boil, stirring to dissolve the sugar and salt. Pour the mixture into a large mason jar and add the thyme, garlic, and bay leaves.

2 Warm a large cast-iron skillet over high heat for 5 minutes.

3 Spray the skillet with nonstick cooking spray and add the jalapeños. Weigh them down with a smaller pan and cook until charred, about 5 minutes.

4 Place the jalapeños in the brine, add the carrots to the skillet, and weigh them down with the smaller pan. Cook until charred, add them to the brine, and let the mixture cool to room temperature before covering and storing in the refrigerator. Let sit for at least 1 day before serving. To can the escabeche, see page 325.

PAIRS WELL WITH: SEAFOOD, AUTUMN-THEMED BOARDS, SPICED NUTS

FRIED

Mustard Greens

YIELD: 4 SERVINGS / **ACTIVE TIME:** 20 MINUTES / **TOTAL TIME:** 30 MINUTES

INGREDIENTS

1 bunch of mustard greens

4 cups canola oil

Salt, to taste

1   Remove the mustard green leaves from their stems and rinse them well. Pat them dry with paper towels and set them aside.

2   Place the canola oil in a wide and deep cast-iron skillet and warm it to 300°F over medium heat. Add the greens and fry, turning them over once, until crispy, 1 to 2 minutes. Remove with a slotted spoon, place them on a paper towel–lined plate to drain, and season with salt. Serve once they have cooled slightly.

PAIRS WELL WITH: SPICY FOODS, FRUIT, GOAT CHEESE

STUFFED
Prunes

YIELD: 4 SERVINGS / **ACTIVE TIME:** 10 MINUTES / **TOTAL TIME:** 10 MINUTES

INGREDIENTS

15 dried prunes

3 oz. blue cheese, crumbled

1 Cut a slit in the top of each prune, stuff them with the blue cheese, and either serve immediately or chill in the refrigerator. If refrigerating, let the stuffed prunes come to room temperature before serving.

PAIRS WELL WITH: NUTS, SALAMI, FRUIT

DUXELLES

INGREDIENTS

1 tablespoon extra-virgin olive oil

3 portobello mushrooms, finely diced

½ shallot, minced

2 tablespoons fresh thyme, chopped

Salt and pepper, to taste

1 Place the olive oil in a large skillet and warm it over medium heat. When the oil starts to shimmer, add the mushrooms and cook, stirring frequently, until they have released all of their liquid and start to brown, about 8 minutes.

2 Stir in the shallot and thyme, cook, stirring occasionally, for 2 minutes, and transfer the mixture to a food processor. Pulse until the desired texture has been achieved.

3 Season with salt and pepper and serve.

PAIRS WELL WITH: CURED MEATS, BLUE CHEESES, PICKLED VEGETABLES

PICKLED
Red Onion

YIELD: 4 SERVINGS / ACTIVE TIME: 15 MINUTES / TOTAL TIME: 4 HOURS AND 30 MINUTES

INGREDIENTS

1 red onion, sliced thin

1 tablespoon black peppercorns

Pinch of kosher salt

1 cup red wine

1 cup red wine vinegar

1 cup sugar

1 Place the onion, peppercorns, and salt in a large mason jar.

2 Combine the wine, vinegar, and sugar in a saucepan and bring the mixture to a boil, stirring to dissolve the sugar.

3 Pour the brine into the mason jar and let it cool to room temperature. To can the pickled onion, see page 325. If not, chill in the refrigerator for at least 4 hours before serving.

PAIRS WELL WITH: SPICY FOODS, CREAMY DIPS, SMOKED MEATS

TAPENADE

YIELD: ½ CUP / **ACTIVE TIME:** 10 MINUTES / **TOTAL TIME:** 10 MINUTES

INGREDIENTS

½ cup finely chopped Kalamata olives

1 teaspoon capers, drained, rinsed, and finely chopped

1 teaspoon finely chopped sun-dried tomatoes in olive oil

1 teaspoon dried oregano

1 Combine the ingredients in a mixing bowl and serve immediately.

PAIRS WELL WITH: FLATBREADS, SPICY FOODS, BUTTERY CHEESES

EGGPLANT
Rings

YIELD: 4 SERVINGS / **ACTIVE TIME:** 40 MINUTES / **TOTAL TIME:** 1 HOUR

INGREDIENTS

1 large eggplant, trimmed and sliced

2 eggs, beaten

1 cup all-purpose flour

1 cup panko

1 tablespoon kosher salt

1 tablespoon black pepper

Canola oil, as needed

¼ cup Red Zhug (see page 174)

¼ cup ketchup

1. Cut the centers out of the slices of eggplant, creating rings that have about an inch of eggplant inside.

2. Place the eggs, flour, and panko in separate bowls. Add the salt and pepper to the bowl of panko and stir to combine. Dredge an eggplant ring in the flour, then the eggs, followed by the panko, until the ring is entirely coated. Place the coated rings on a baking sheet.

3. Add canola oil to a cast-iron skillet until it is about 1 inch deep and warm to 375°F over medium-high heat. Working in batches to avoid crowding the pan, gently lay the eggplant rings in the oil and cook until browned and crispy all over, about 4 minutes, turning as necessary. Place the cooked rings on a paper towel–lined plate to drain.

4. Place the zhug and ketchup in a small bowl, stir to combine, and serve alongside the eggplant rings.

PAIRS WELL WITH: SPICY CONDIMENTS, MEDITERRANEAN-THEMED BOARDS, SHARP CHEESES

CORN

Fritters

YIELD: 4 SERVINGS / **ACTIVE TIME:** 20 MINUTES / **TOTAL TIME:** 40 MINUTES

INGREDIENTS

1 egg, beaten

1 teaspoon sugar

½ teaspoon kosher salt

1 tablespoon unsalted butter, melted

2 teaspoons baking powder

1 cup all-purpose flour

⅔ cup milk

2 cups corn kernels, at room temperature

¼ cup extra-virgin olive oil

1   Place the egg, sugar, salt, butter, baking powder, flour, and milk in a mixing bowl and stir until thoroughly combined. Add the corn and stir to incorporate.

2   Place the oil in a 12-inch cast-iron skillet and warm over medium-high heat. When the oil starts to shimmer, drop heaping tablespoons of batter into the skillet and gently press down to flatten them into disks. Work in batches to avoid crowding the pan. Cook until the fritters are browned on both sides, about 3 minutes per side. Transfer to a paper towel–lined plate and tent with aluminum foil to keep warm while you cook the rest of the fritters. Serve once all the fritters have been cooked.

PAIRS WELL WITH: SPICY & CREAMY DIPS, SUMMER-THEMED BOARDS

BLISTERED
Shishito Peppers

YIELD: 6 SERVINGS / ACTIVE TIME: 5 MINUTES / TOTAL TIME: 10 MINUTES

INGREDIENTS

Extra-virgin olive oil, as needed

2 lbs. shishito peppers

Salt, to taste

1 lemon, cut into wedges

1 Add olive oil to a 12-inch cast-iron skillet until it is ¼ inch deep and warm over medium heat.

2 When the oil is shimmering, add the peppers and cook, while turning once or twice, until they are blistered and golden brown, about 10 minutes. Take care not to crowd the pan with the peppers, working in batches if necessary.

3 Transfer the blistered peppers to a paper towel–lined plate. Season with salt and squeeze the lemon wedges over them before serving.

PAIRS WELL WITH: MEXICAN-STYLE LAGERS, POULTRY, SPICY FOODS

STUFFED
Mushrooms

YIELD: 8 SERVINGS / ACTIVE TIME: 30 MINUTES / TOTAL TIME: 1 HOUR AND 30 MINUTES

INGREDIENTS

10 oz. button mushrooms, stemmed

¼ cup extra-virgin olive oil, plus more as needed

3 tablespoons balsamic vinegar

Salt and pepper, to taste

8 oz. ground Italian sausage

2 yellow onions, grated

5 garlic cloves, grated

8 oz. cream cheese, softened

1 cup shredded Asiago cheese

1 Place the mushrooms, olive oil, and balsamic vinegar in a mixing bowl and toss to coat. Season the mixture with salt and pepper and then place it on a baking sheet. Place in the oven and bake until the mushrooms are just starting to brown, about 25 minutes. Remove from the oven and set them aside.

2 Coat the bottom of a large skillet with olive oil and warm it over medium heat. When the oil starts to shimmer, add the sausage and cook, breaking it up with a fork as it browns, until cooked through, about 8 minutes. Remove the sausage from the pan and place it in a mixing bowl.

3 Preheat the oven to 375°F. Place the onions in the skillet, reduce the heat to medium-low, and cook until dark brown, about 15 minutes. Stir in the garlic, sauté for 1 minute, and then add the mixture to the bowl containing the sausage. Add the cheeses to the bowl containing the sausage and stir to combine.

4 Arrange the mushrooms on the baking sheet so that their cavities are facing up. Fill the cavities with the sausage mixture, place the mushrooms in the oven, and bake until the cheese has melted and is golden brown, about 25 minutes. Remove from the oven and let cool slightly before serving.

PAIRS WELL WITH: BLUE CHEESES, HOLIDAY-THEMED BOARDS

TIROPITAKIA

YIELD: 6 SERVINGS / **ACTIVE TIME:** 45 MINUTES / **TOTAL TIME:** 1 HOUR AND 15 MINUTES

INGREDIENTS

8 oz. feta cheese

1 cup grated kefalotyri cheese

¼ cup chopped fresh parsley

2 eggs, beaten

Black pepper, to taste

1 (1 lb.) package of frozen phyllo dough, thawed

8 oz. unsalted butter, melted

1 Place the feta in a mixing bowl and break it up with a fork. Add the kefalotyri, parsley, eggs, and pepper and stir to combine. Set the mixture aside.

2 Place 1 sheet of the phyllo dough on a large sheet of parchment paper. Gently brush the sheet with some of the melted butter, place another sheet on top, and brush this with more of the butter. Cut the phyllo dough into 2-inch-wide strips, place 1 teaspoon of the filling at the end of the strip closest to you, and fold one corner over to make a triangle. Fold the strip up until the filling is completely covered. Repeat with the remaining sheets of phyllo dough and filling.

3 Preheat the oven to 350°F and coat a baking sheet with some of the melted butter. Place the pastries on the baking sheet and bake in the oven until golden brown, about 15 minutes. Remove and let cool briefly before serving.

PAIRS WELL WITH: CREAMY DIPS, MEDITERRANEAN-THEMED BOARDS, OLIVES

SCALLION
Pancakes

YIELD: 6 SERVINGS / **ACTIVE TIME:** 40 MINUTES / **TOTAL TIME:** 1 HOUR AND 15 MINUTES

INGREDIENTS

1½ cups all-purpose flour, plus more as needed

¾ cup boiling water

7 tablespoons canola oil

1 tablespoon toasted sesame oil

1 teaspoon kosher salt

4 scallions, trimmed and sliced thin

1 Place the flour and water in a mixing bowl and work the mixture until it comes together as a rough dough. Transfer the dough to a flour-dusted work surface and knead it until it is a tacky, nearly smooth ball. Cover the dough with plastic wrap and let it rest for 30 minutes.

2 Place 1 tablespoon of the canola oil, the sesame oil, and 1 tablespoon of flour in a small bowl and stir to combine. Set the mixture aside.

3 Divide the dough in half, cover one piece with plastic wrap, and set it aside. Place the other piece on a flour-dusted work surface and roll it into a 12-inch round. Drizzle approximately 1 tablespoon of the oil-and-flour mixture over the round and use a pastry brush to spread the mixture evenly. Sprinkle half of the salt and scallions over the round and roll it into a cylinder. Coil the cylinder into a spiral and flatten it with your palm. Cover with plastic wrap and repeat with the other piece of dough.

4 Warm a cast-iron skillet over low heat until it is warm. Roll one piece of dough into a 9-inch round and make a slit, approximately ½ inch deep, in the center of the round. Cover with plastic wrap and repeat with the other piece of dough.

5 Coat the bottom of the skillet with some of the remaining canola oil and raise the heat to medium-low. When the oil is warm, place 1 pancake in the pan, cover it, and cook until the pancake is golden brown, about 1 minute. Drizzle some sesame oil over the pancake, use a pastry brush to spread it evenly, and carefully flip the pancake over.

6 Cover the pan and cook until the pancake is browned on that side, about 1 minute. Remove the cover and cook the pancake until it is crisp and a deep golden brown, about 30 seconds. Remove and cook until crispy on that side, another 30 seconds. Remove from the pan, transfer to a wire rack to cool, and cook the other pancake. When both pancakes have been cooked, slice each one into wedges and serve.

PAIRS WELL WITH: SPICY DIPS, SEAFOOD, CURED MEATS

KALE Chips

YIELD: 4 SERVINGS / ACTIVE TIME: 5 MINUTES / TOTAL TIME: 15 MINUTES

INGREDIENTS

1 bunch of kale, stemmed

1 teaspoon kosher salt

½ teaspoon black pepper

½ teaspoon paprika

½ teaspoon dried parsley

½ teaspoon dried basil

¼ teaspoon dried thyme

¼ teaspoon dried sage

2 tablespoons extra-virgin olive oil

1   Preheat the oven to 400°F. Tear the kale leaves into smaller pieces and place them in a mixing bowl. Add the remaining ingredients and work the mixture with your hands until the kale pieces are evenly coated.

2   Divide the seasoned kale between two parchment-lined baking sheets so that it sits on each in an even layer. Place in the oven and bake until crispy, 6 to 8 minutes. Remove and let cool before serving.

PAIRS WELL WITH: VEGAN, VEGETARIAN & AUTUMN-THEMED BOARDS

TURKISH EGGPLANT
Salad

YIELD: 4 SERVINGS / **ACTIVE TIME:** 20 MINUTES / **TOTAL TIME:** 1 HOUR AND 30 MINUTES

INGREDIENTS

2 large eggplants

2 tablespoons extra-virgin olive oil

3 medium tomatoes, diced

1 white onion, julienned

4 garlic cloves, minced

1 tablespoon paprika

1 teaspoon kosher salt

1 teaspoon cumin

1 teaspoon cayenne pepper

½ cup chopped fresh parsley

1 Preheat the oven to 450°F. Poke a few holes in the eggplants, place them on a baking sheet, and place them in the oven. Roast until completely tender and starting to collapse, 40 minutes to 1 hour. Remove the eggplants from the oven and let them cool completely.

2 Place the oil in a large skillet and warm it over high heat. Add the tomatoes and onion and cook until the onion is translucent, about 4 minutes. Add the remaining ingredients, except for the parsley, and cook for approximately 20 minutes, stirring occasionally. Transfer the mixture to a mixing bowl.

3 Halve the eggplants and scoop the flesh into the tomato mixture. Stir to combine, adding the parsley as you go. Let the mixture cool to room temperature before serving.

PAIRS WELL WITH: FLATBREADS, CRUDITÉS, MEDITERRANEAN-THEMED BOARDS

FRIED
Artichokes

YIELD: 8 SERVINGS / **ACTIVE TIME:** 1 HOUR AND 15 MINUTES / **TOTAL TIME:** 2 HOURS

1   Prepare an ice bath in a large bowl. Squeeze two lemons into the ice bath, stir, and then throw the spent lemon halves into the ice bath. This lemon water will keep the artichokes fresh and green until you're ready to fry them. Keep a couple of fresh lemon halves on hand as you prep.

2   Rinse the artichokes under cold water. Pat them dry with a linen towel or paper towels. Using kitchen shears, remove the thorny tips from the leaves. For each artichoke, remove the bitter, fibrous end of the stem with a knife, leaving about 1½ inches of stem attached to each artichoke.

3   Using a serrated knife, peel the outer skin from the remaining stem. As the stem is more bitter than the rest of the artichoke, removing the skin tempers the bitterness. Rub the peeled stem with fresh lemon to keep it from browning.

4   Peel off 5 or 6 layers of external leaves from each artichoke, snapping off the leaves and setting them aside, until you reach inner leaves that are fresh looking and white at their base.

5   Using a serrated knife or sharp chef's knife, slice each artichoke horizontally, about ¾ inch above the base (aka the heart), and remove the pointy top of the artichoke, leaving a flat crown of leaves at the base of the artichoke while exposing the purple inner leaves.

6   Slice the artichokes in half lengthwise, splitting the stem and heart to reveal the fuzzy choke.

7   Scoop out the white spines and purple leaves from each artichoke half with a melon baller, leaving two hollowed-out halves of the heart with a small crown of flat leaves.

8   Rub the artichokes with lemon and place them in the ice bath.

9   Remove the artichoke halves from the lemon water. Pour the ice bath and spent lemon halves into a large saucepan. You will need about 1½ inches of water to steam the artichokes, so add more water if needed.

10 Place a steamer basket inside the pan and bring the water to a boil. Place the cleaned artichoke halves in the steamer basket and cover the pan. Reduce the heat to medium and steam the artichokes until the thickest part of the stem is just tender, 15 to 20 minutes. You want the artichokes to still be a bit firm—they should only be partially cooked.

11 Place the steamed artichokes on a paper towel–lined plate and let them dry completely.

12 Add avocado oil to a cast-iron skillet until it is 1 inch deep and warm it to 325°F. Season the artichokes with salt and pepper, making sure to season between the layers of leaves as well.

13 Gently slip the artichokes into the hot oil and fry them until the leaves are crispy and golden brown, about 15 minutes, turning the artichokes over halfway through.

14 Remove the artichokes from the oil, transfer to a paper towel–lined plate, and let them drain before serving.

PAIRS WELL WITH: NUTTY CHEESES, CURED MEATS, CREAMY DIPS

INGREDIENTS

5 lemons, halved

4 large artichokes

Avocado oil, as needed

Salt and pepper, to taste

PICKLED
Green Tomatoes

YIELD: 2 PINTS / **ACTIVE TIME:** 15 MINUTES / **TOTAL TIME:** 24 HOURS

INGREDIENTS

1½ cups apple cider vinegar

¾ cup water

2 teaspoons sugar

½ teaspoon whole black peppercorns

½ teaspoon coriander seeds

½ teaspoon caraway seeds

½ teaspoon cumin seeds

3 allspice berries

2 bay leaves

2 tablespoons kosher salt

1 lb. small green tomatoes, sliced

¼ white onion, sliced thin

1   Combine the vinegar, water, sugar, spices, and salt in a saucepan. Bring the mixture to a boil, stirring to dissolve the sugar.

2   Place the tomatoes and onion in a large mason jar and pour the brine over the vegetables. Let the mixture cool completely.

3   To can the tomatoes, see page 325. If not canning, cover and store in the refrigerator overnight before enjoying.

PAIRS WELL WITH: SPICY FOODS, SUMMER-THEMED BOARDS

KEFTES
de Espinaca

YIELD: 12 SERVINGS / **ACTIVE TIME:** 15 MINUTES / **TOTAL TIME:** 30 MINUTES

INGREDIENTS

½ cup avocado oil, plus 1 tablespoon

1 onion, minced

½ teaspoon grated garlic

10 oz. fresh spinach

1 large egg

1 cup mashed russet potatoes

½ cup plain bread crumbs

1 teaspoon fine sea salt

¼ teaspoon black pepper

Pinch of cayenne pepper

1 Place the 1 tablespoon of avocado oil in a large skillet and warm it over medium heat. Add the onion and cook, stirring frequently, until it starts to soften, about 5 minutes.

2 Add the garlic and cook until fragrant, about 1 minute. Add half of the spinach, cover the pan, and cook until the spinach has wilted. Add the remaining spinach, cover the pan again, and cook until all of the spinach has wilted.

3 Transfer the mixture to a fine-mesh strainer and gently press down on the mixture to remove excess moisture. Transfer the mixture to a cutting board and roughly chop it.

4 Place the mixture in a mixing bowl. Add the remaining ingredients and stir until thoroughly combined. Form ¼-cup portions of the mixture into patties and place them on a parchment-lined baking sheet.

5 Place the remaining oil in the skillet and warm it to 365°F. Working in batches to avoid crowding the pan, slip the patties into the hot oil and fry until brown on both sides, about 8 minutes. Transfer the keftes to a paper towel–lined plate to drain before serving.

PAIRS WELL WITH: SPICY DIPS, VEGAN & VEGETARIAN BOARDS, MEDITERRANEAN-THEMED BOARDS

MARINATED
Olives

YIELD: 8 SERVINGS / **ACTIVE TIME:** 20 MINUTES / **TOTAL TIME:** 2 HOURS AND 30 MINUTES

INGREDIENTS

1½ lbs. assorted olives

2 teaspoons lightly cracked
coriander seeds

1 teaspoon lightly cracked fennel
seeds

¾ cup extra-virgin olive oil

2 tablespoons red wine vinegar

4 garlic cloves, sliced thin

1½ teaspoons chopped rosemary

1½ teaspoons thyme

4 bay leaves, torn

1 small dried red chile pepper,
stem and seeds removed, chopped

2 strips of lemon zest

1 Rinse any dark olives under cold water so their juices don't discolor the other olives. Place all of the olives in a colander and drain them. Transfer the olives to a wide-mouthed jar and set them aside.

2 Warm a dry skillet over medium-high heat. Add the coriander and fennel seeds and toast until very fragrant, about 2 minutes, stirring occasionally. Add the olive oil and vinegar and cook for 1 minute.

3 Remove the pan from heat and add all the remaining ingredients. Stir to combine and let the mixture cool completely.

4 Pour the marinade over the olives, cover, and shake the jar to coat the olives.

5 Chill the olives in the refrigerator for 2 hours before serving. If preparing the olives a few days ahead of time, shake the jar daily to redistribute the seasonings.

PAIRS WELL WITH: DRY WHITE WINES, CURED MEATS, FLATBREADS

ROASTED PLUMS WITH
Tahini Dressing

YIELD: 4 SERVINGS / ACTIVE TIME: 20 MINUTES / TOTAL TIME: 2 HOURS AND 30 MINUTES

INGREDIENTS

2 lbs. plums, halved and pitted

2 tablespoons avocado oil

1½ teaspoons fine sea salt, plus more to taste

¼ teaspoon black pepper

1 tablespoon fresh thyme or oregano

3 tablespoons fresh lemon juice, plus more to taste

1 cup tahini

1 ice cube

Flaky sea salt (Maldon recommended), to taste

1 Preheat the oven to 400°F and line a baking sheet with parchment paper. Arrange the plums, cut side up, on the baking sheet, drizzle the avocado oil over them, and sprinkle the fine sea salt, pepper, and herbs over them. Toss to coat.

2 Place the baking sheet in the oven and reduce the heat to 250°F. Roast until the plums are very soft and starting to caramelize, about 2 hours. Remove the plums from the oven and let them cool slightly.

3 Place the lemon juice, tahini, ¾ cup water, a few pinches of salt, and the ice cube in a mixing bowl and whisk vigorously until the dressing comes together. It should lighten in color and thicken enough that it holds an edge when the whisk is dragged through it. Remove the ice cube, if any of it remains, taste, and adjust the seasoning as necessary.

4 Arrange the plums on a plate, drizzle the dressing over the top, and sprinkle the flaky sea salt—preferably Maldon—over the top.

PAIRS WELL WITH: GAME MEATS, NUTS, CREAMY CHEESES

OKRA & LEMONS
with Za'atar

YIELD: 4 SERVINGS / **ACTIVE TIME:** 20 MINUTES / **TOTAL TIME:** 20 MINUTES

INGREDIENTS

2 tablespoons avocado oil

1 lb. okra, trimmed

1 lemon, cut into wedges

Salt, to taste

Za'atar seasoning, to taste

Fresh parsley, chopped, for garnish

1 Place the avocado oil in a large skillet and warm it over high heat. Add the okra and lemon wedges, season with salt, and cook, stirring frequently, until the okra and lemon begin to char.

2 Remove the pan from heat, stir in the za'atar, and then remove the pan from heat. Place the mixture in a serving bowl, garnish with parsley, and enjoy.

PAIRS WELL WITH: SPICY FOODS, MEDITERRANEAN-THEMED BOARDS, SEAFOOD

SOMETHING SWEET

Savory is far and away the most popular flavor on a serving board, but that just means there's always room for something sweet. Whether it be a cookie platter at a holiday party or a collection of small bites to send around after dinner, these treats promise to take any gathering to the next level.

CHOCOLATE CHIP
Cookies

YIELD: 16 COOKIES / **ACTIVE TIME:** 15 MINUTES / **TOTAL TIME:** 45 MINUTES

INGREDIENTS

7 oz. unsalted butter

8¾ oz. all-purpose flour

½ teaspoon baking soda

3½ oz. sugar

5⅓ oz. dark brown sugar

1 teaspoon fine sea salt

2 teaspoons pure vanilla extract

1 large egg

1 large egg yolk

1¼ cups semisweet chocolate chips

1 Preheat the oven to 350°F. Place the butter in a saucepan and cook over medium-high heat until it is starting to brown and give off a nutty aroma (let your nose guide you here, making sure you frequently waft the steam toward you). Transfer to a heatproof mixing bowl.

2 Place the flour and baking soda in a bowl and whisk until combined.

3 Add the sugars, salt, and vanilla to the bowl containing the melted butter and whisk until combined. Add the egg and egg yolk and whisk until the mixture is smooth and thick. Add the flour-and-baking soda mixture and stir until incorporated. Add the chocolate chips and stir until evenly distributed. Form the mixture into 16 balls and place on parchment-lined baking sheets, leaving about 2 inches between each ball.

4 Working with one baking sheet at a time, place it in the oven and bake until golden brown, 12 to 16 minutes, rotating the sheet halfway through the bake time. Remove from the oven and let cool to room temperature before serving.

PAIRS WELL WITH: DESSERT & HOLIDAY BOARDS

CLASSIC SUGAR
Cookies

YIELD: 48 COOKIES / **ACTIVE TIME:** 40 MINUTES / **TOTAL TIME:** 3 HOURS

INGREDIENTS

8 oz. unsalted butter, softened

7 oz. light brown sugar

1 egg

12 oz. all-purpose flour, plus more as needed

1 teaspoon baking powder

½ teaspoon kosher salt

1   In the work bowl of a stand mixer fitted with the paddle attachment, cream the butter and brown sugar on medium speed until the mixture is very light and fluffy, about 5 minutes. Scrape down the work bowl and then beat the mixture for another 5 minutes.

2   Reduce the speed to low, add the egg, and beat until incorporated. Scrape down the work bowl and beat the mixture for 1 minute on medium.

3   Add the remaining ingredients, reduce the speed to low, and beat until the mixture comes together as a dough. Form the dough into a ball and then flatten it into a disk. Cover the dough in plastic wrap and refrigerate for 2 hours.

4   Preheat the oven to 350°F and line two baking sheets with parchment paper.

5   Remove the dough from the refrigerator and let it sit on the counter for 5 minutes.

6   Place the dough on a flour-dusted work surface and roll it out until it is approximately ¼ inch thick. Use cookie cutters to cut the dough into the desired shapes and place them on the baking sheets. Form any scraps into a ball, roll it out, and cut into cookies. If the dough becomes too sticky or warm, place it back in the refrigerator for 15 minutes to firm up.

7   Place the cookies in the oven and bake until lightly golden brown at their edges, 8 to 10 minutes. Remove from the oven, transfer to a wire rack, and let cool for 10 minutes before enjoying or decorating.

PAIRS WELL WITH: BRUNCH, DESSERT & HOLIDAY BOARDS

SNICKERDOODLES

YIELD: 24 COOKIES / **ACTIVE TIME:** 25 MINUTES / **TOTAL TIME:** 1 HOUR

INGREDIENTS

15 oz. all-purpose flour

2 teaspoons cream of tartar

1 teaspoon baking soda

2½ teaspoons cinnamon

½ teaspoon kosher salt

8 oz. unsalted butter, softened

11⅔ oz. sugar

1 large egg, at room temperature

2 teaspoons pure vanilla extract

1 Preheat the oven to 375°F and line two baking sheets with parchment paper. Whisk together the flour, cream of tartar, baking soda, 1½ teaspoons of the cinnamon, and the salt together in a mixing bowl.

2 In the work bowl of a stand mixer fitted with the paddle attachment, cream the butter and all but 2 oz. of the sugar together on medium speed until light and fluffy. Add the egg and vanilla and beat until combined, scraping down the work bowl as needed. With the mixer running on low, add the dry mixture in three increments, waiting until each portion has been incorporated until adding the next. The mixture will come together as a thick dough.

3 Roll tablespoons of the dough into balls. Place the remaining cinnamon and sugar in a mixing bowl and stir to combine. Roll the balls in the mixture until coated and place them on the baking sheets.

4 Place in the oven and bake for 10 minutes, until puffy and very soft. Remove from the oven, press down with a spatula to flatten them out, and let cool on the baking sheets for 10 minutes before transferring to a wire rack to cool completely.

PAIRS WELL WITH: DESSERT BOARDS

MACARONS

YIELD: 30 MACARONS / **ACTIVE TIME:** 45 MINUTES / **TOTAL TIME:** 4 HOURS

INGREDIENTS

11 oz. fine almond flour

11 oz. confectioners' sugar

8 egg whites

Pinch of fine sea salt

11 oz. sugar

½ cup water

2 to 3 drops of gel food coloring (optional)

1 Place the almond flour and confectioners' sugar in a food processor and blitz for about 1 minute, until the mixture is thoroughly combined and has a fine texture. Place the mixture in a mixing bowl, add three of the egg whites and the salt, and stir with a rubber spatula until the mixture is almost a paste. Set the mixture aside.

2 Place the sugar and water in a small saucepan. Fit the saucepan with a candy thermometer and cook the mixture over high heat.

3 While the syrup is coming to a boil, wipe out the work bowl of the stand mixer, place the remaining egg whites in it, and whip on medium until they hold firm peaks.

4 Cook the syrup until it is 245°F. Remove the pan from heat and carefully add the syrup to the whipped egg whites, slowly pouring it down the side of the work bowl. When all the syrup has been added, whip the mixture until it is glossy, holds stiff peaks, and has cooled slightly. If desired, stir in the food coloring.

5 Add half of the meringue to the almond flour mixture and fold to incorporate. Fold in the remaining meringue. When incorporated, the batter should be smooth, very glossy, and not too runny.

6 Line two baking sheets with parchment paper. Fit a piping bag with a plain tip and fill it with the batter. Pipe evenly sized rounds onto the baking sheets, leaving an inch of space between each one. You want the rounds to be about the size of a silver dollar (approximately 2 inches wide) when you pipe them onto the sheet; they will spread slightly as they sit.

7 Gently tap each sheet pan to smooth the tops of the macarons.

8 Let the macarons sit at room temperature, uncovered, for 1 hour. This allows a skin to form on them.

9 Preheat the oven to 325°F.

10 Place the macarons in the oven and bake for 10 minutes. Rotate the baking sheets and let them bake for another 5 minutes. Turn off the oven, crack the oven door, and let the macarons sit in the oven for 5 minutes.

11 Remove the cookies from the oven and let them sit on a cooling rack for 2 hours. When the macarons are completely cool, fill as desired.

PAIRS WELL WITH: BRUNCH & DESSERT BOARDS, MILD & CREAMY CHEESES

FILLINGS

The macaron can accommodate a large number of fillings, and thus appeal to a wide spectrum of palates. While you shouldn't be afraid to be bold with your filling decisions, always remember to err on the dry side, as wetter fillings, such as whipped cream, will dissolve the cookie. To get your mind working, here are a few standard fillings.

Chocolate Ganache: Heat ½ cup heavy cream in a saucepan and bring to a simmer. Stir in ¼ pound of chopped dark chocolate and continue stirring until the chocolate is melted. Add 2 tablespoons unsalted butter, stir until the mixture is smooth, and chill in the refrigerator until thick and cool.

Vanilla Buttercream: Place 10 tablespoons unsalted butter in a mixing bowl and beat at medium speed with a handheld mixer fitted with a whisk attachment until smooth. Add 1½ teaspoons pure vanilla extract, 1¼ cups confectioners' sugar, and a pinch of kosher salt and beat until the mixture is fully combined. Scrape down the bowl as needed while mixing. Add 1 tablespoon heavy cream and beat until the mixture is light and fluffy, about 4 minutes, stopping to scrape down the bowl as needed.

Raspberry Buttercream: Add ¼ cup of seedless raspberry jam to the Vanilla Buttercream and beat until incorporated.

Lemon Curd: Place 1 cup fresh lemon juice, 4 teaspoons of lemon zest, 6 large eggs, 1⅓ cups sugar, and 2 sticks of unsalted butter in the work bowl of a stand mixer fitted with the paddle attachment. Beat on medium speed until well combined. Pour the mixture into a saucepan and cook over low heat until it is thick enough to coat the back of a wooden spoon, about 10 minutes. Pour the lemon curd into a bowl, place it in the refrigerator, and chill until it thickens to a custard-like consistency.

MACARONS
SEE PAGE 392

COCONUT
Macaroons

YIELD: 12 MACAROONS / ACTIVE TIME: 45 MINUTES / TOTAL TIME: 3 HOURS

INGREDIENTS

1 (14 oz.) can of sweetened condensed milk

7 oz. sweetened shredded coconut

7 oz. unsweetened shredded coconut

¼ teaspoon kosher salt

½ teaspoon pure vanilla extract

2 egg whites

Chocolate Ganache (see page 393), warm

1 Line a baking sheet with parchment paper. In a mixing bowl, add the sweetened condensed milk, shredded coconut, salt, and vanilla and stir with a rubber spatula until combined. Set the mixture aside.

2 In the work bowl of a stand mixer fitted with the whisk attachment, whip the egg whites until they hold stiff peaks. Add the whipped egg whites to the coconut mixture and fold to incorporate.

3 Scoop 2-oz. portions of the mixture onto the baking sheet, making sure to leave enough space between them. Place the baking sheet in the refrigerator and let the dough firm up for 1 hour.

4 Preheat the oven to 350°F.

5 Place the cookies in the oven and bake until they are lightly golden brown, 20 to 25 minutes.

6 Remove the cookies from the oven, transfer them to a cooling rack, and let them cool for 1 hour.

7 If desired, dip the bottoms of the macaroons into the ganache and then place them back on the baking sheet. Drizzle some of the ganache over the tops of the cookies. Refrigerate until the chocolate is set, about 5 minutes, before serving.

PAIRS WELL WITH: SUMMER-THEMED & DESSERT BOARDS

ORANGE
Spritz

YIELD: 48 COOKIES / **ACTIVE TIME:** 15 MINUTES / **TOTAL TIME:** 45 MINUTES

INGREDIENTS

8 oz. unsalted butter, softened

7 oz. sugar

1 tablespoon light brown sugar

Zest of 1 orange

2 egg yolks

11¼ oz. all-purpose flour

¼ teaspoon fine sea salt

¼ teaspoon baking soda

Confectioners' sugar, for dusting

1 Preheat the oven to 350°F and line two baking sheets with parchment paper. Place the butter, sugars, and orange zest in the work bowl of a stand mixer fitted with the paddle attachment and cream the mixture until pale and fluffy, scraping down the sides of the bowl as needed.

2 Add the egg yolks and beat until incorporated. Sift the flour, salt, and baking soda into a separate mixing bowl. Gradually add the dry mixture to the butter mixture and work the mixture with your hands until it comes together as a smooth dough.

3 Shape the dough into small logs, place them in a cookie press, and press the desired shapes onto the baking sheets.

4 Place the cookies in the oven and bake for 10 to 12 minutes, until the edges start to brown. Remove from the oven and transfer the cookies to wire racks to cool. Dust with confectioners' sugar before serving.

PAIRS WELL WITH: DESSERT & HOLIDAY BOARDS

CLASSIC GINGERBREAD
Cookies

YIELD: 24 COOKIES / **ACTIVE TIME:** 20 MINUTES / **ACTIVE TIME:** 2 HOURS

INGREDIENTS

6 oz. unsalted butter, softened

3½ oz. light brown sugar

⅔ cup molasses

1 large egg, at room temperature

1 teaspoon baking soda

1 teaspoon ground ginger

1 teaspoon apple pie spice

½ teaspoon fine sea salt

½ teaspoon pure vanilla extract

¼ teaspoon freshly ground black pepper

3 cups all-purpose flour, plus more as needed

1 Place the butter and brown sugar in the work bowl of a stand mixer fitted with the paddle attachment and beat at low speed until combined. Increase the speed to high and beat until the mixture is light and fluffy. Add the molasses, egg, baking soda, ginger, apple pie spice, salt, vanilla, and pepper and beat for 1 minute. Slowly add the flour to the mixture and beat until it comes together as a stiff dough.

2 Divide the dough in half and wrap each half in plastic wrap. Flatten each piece into a disk and refrigerate for 1 hour. The dough will keep in the refrigerator for up to 2 days.

3 Preheat the oven to 350°F and line two baking sheets with parchment paper. Place the dough on a flour-dusted work surface and roll to a thickness of ¼ inch. Dip cookie cutters in flour and cut the dough into desired shapes. Transfer the cookies to the baking sheets and bake until firm, about 10 minutes.

4 Remove cookies from oven, let rest for 2 minutes, and then set on wire racks to cool completely. Decorate as desired and enjoy.

PAIRS WELL WITH: DESSERT & HOLIDAY BOARDS

POLVORONES

YIELD: 36 COOKIES / **ACTIVE TIME:** 20 MINUTES / **TOTAL TIME:** 1 HOUR

INGREDIENTS

8 oz. unsalted butter, softened

7 oz. confectioners' sugar

4 oz. cake flour, plus more for dusting

5 oz. self-rising flour

1 cup almonds, blanched and minced

½ teaspoon pure vanilla extract

Warm water (110°F), as needed

1   Preheat the oven to 350°F and line two baking sheets with parchment paper. Place the butter and 5 oz. of the confectioners' sugar in the work bowl of a stand mixer fitted with the paddle attachment and cream until light and fluffy. Add the flours, almonds, and vanilla and beat until the mixture comes together as a very stiff dough. Add a few drops of warm water, if necessary, to make it pliable.

2   Form tablespoons of the dough into balls. Place the balls on the baking sheets and flatten them slightly with the bottom of a glass that has been dipped in flour.

3   Place the cookies in the oven and bake until lightly browned, about 10 minutes.

4   Remove the cookies from the oven. Sift the remaining sugar into a shallow bowl and roll the cookies in the sugar until they are evenly coated. Transfer them to wire racks to cool completely.

PAIRS WELL WITH: DESSERT & HOLIDAY BOARDS, NUTS

TORCETTI
di Saint Vincent

YIELD: 24 COOKIES / **ACTIVE TIME:** 45 MINUTES / **TOTAL TIME:** 3 HOURS

INGREDIENTS

½ cup warm water (105°F)

1¼ teaspoons active dry yeast

7½ oz. all-purpose flour, plus more as needed

¼ teaspoon fine sea salt

1¼ oz. unsalted butter, chilled

¼ cup sugar

1   Place the water and yeast in a mixing bowl and gently stir to combine. Let the mixture sit until it becomes foamy, about 10 minutes.

2   In a mixing bowl, combine the flour and salt. Add the butter and work the mixture with your hands until the mixture is fine and crumbly. Stir in the yeast mixture and work the resulting mixture until it comes together as a dough.

3   Place the dough in a greased bowl and roll it around until it is well coated. Cover the bowl with plastic wrap and let the dough rise for 1 hour.

4   Line two baking sheets with parchment paper. Place the dough on a flour-dusted work surface and roll it into a square that is about 3 inches thick. Cut the dough into smaller squares and roll each one until it is 5 inches long and as thin as a pencil.

5   Place the sugar on a plate and roll the pieces of dough in it until completely coated. Form the pieces of dough into loops, place them on the baking sheets, leaving 1½ inches between them, and let them rest for 20 minutes.

6   Preheat the oven to 325°F.

7   Place the cookies in the oven and bake until golden brown, 20 to 25 minutes. Remove from the oven and let cool completely before serving.

PAIRS WELL WITH: BREAKFAST & BRUNCH BOARDS, ITALIAN-THEMED BOARDS

LEMON & ALMOND
Biscotti

YIELD: 24 BISCOTTI / **ACTIVE TIME:** 1 HOUR / **TOTAL TIME:** 4 HOURS AND 30 MINUTES

INGREDIENTS

8 oz. unsalted butter, softened

Zest of 1 lemon

7 oz. sugar

¾ teaspoon pure vanilla extract

2 eggs

10 oz. all-purpose flour

½ teaspoon baking soda

½ teaspoon baking powder

½ teaspoon fine sea salt

8 oz. slivered almonds, toasted

1　Line a baking sheet with parchment paper. In the work bowl of a stand mixer fitted with the paddle attachment, cream the butter, lemon zest, sugar, and vanilla on medium until the mixture is very light and fluffy, about 5 minutes. Scrape down the work bowl and then beat the mixture for another 5 minutes.

2　Add the eggs one at a time and beat on low until incorporated, again scraping the work bowl as needed. When both eggs have been incorporated, scrape down the work bowl and beat on medium for 1 minute.

3　Add the remaining ingredients, reduce the speed to low, and beat until the mixture comes together as a dough.

4　Place the dough on the baking sheet and form it into a log that is the length of the pan and anywhere from 3 to 4 inches wide. Place the dough in the refrigerator for 1 hour.

5　Preheat the oven to 350°F.

6　Place the biscotti dough in the oven and bake until golden brown and a cake tester comes out clean when inserted into the center, 25 to 30 minutes. Remove the biscotti from the oven, transfer it to a cooling rack, and let it cool completely before chilling in the refrigerator for 2 hours.

7　Preheat the oven to 250°F. Cut the biscotti to the desired size, place them on their sides, place in the oven, and bake for 10 minutes. Remove from the oven, turn them over, and bake for another 6 minutes. Remove from the oven and let them cool completely before enjoying.

PAIRS WELL WITH: BREAKFAST & BRUNCH BOARDS, NUTS, MILD & CREAMY CHEESES

LEMON Squares

YIELD: 12 SQUARES / ACTIVE TIME: 15 MINUTES / TOTAL TIME: 1 HOUR

INGREDIENTS

4 oz. unsalted butter

⅓ cup confectioners' sugar

1 cup all-purpose flour, plus 2 tablespoons

Pinch of kosher salt

2 large eggs, at room temperature

1 cup sugar

⅓ cup fresh lemon juice

1 tablespoon lemon zest

1   Preheat the oven to 350°F and coat a square 8-inch cake pan with nonstick cooking spray.

2   Place the butter, ¼ cup of the confectioners' sugar, the 1 cup of flour, and salt in a mixing bowl and stir until combined. Press the mixture into the baking pan and bake for 20 minutes, or until it is set and lightly browned. Remove from the oven and set aside.

3   Place the eggs, sugar, remaining flour, lemon juice, and lemon zest in a mixing bowl and beat with a handheld mixer until thoroughly combined.

4   Pour the custard over the crust and bake for 20 minutes, or until just browned. The custard should still be soft. Let the pan cool on a wire rack before dusting with the remaining confectioners' sugar and cutting into squares.

PAIRS WELL WITH: DESSERT & SUMMER-THEMED BOARDS

MADELEINES

YIELD: 30 MADELEINES / **ACTIVE TIME:** 40 MINUTES / **TOTAL TIME:** 3 HOURS AND 30 MINUTES

INGREDIENTS

8 oz. sugar

8 oz. egg whites

Zest of 1 lemon

3¼ oz. fine almond flour

3¼ oz. all-purpose flour

7 oz. unsalted butter

1 teaspoon pure vanilla extract

Confectioners' sugar, for dusting

1   In the work bowl of a stand mixer fitted with the paddle attachment, beat the sugar, egg whites, and lemon zest on medium until the mixture is light and fluffy. Add the flours and beat until incorporated. Set the mixture aside.

2   Place the butter in a small saucepan and melt it over low heat.

3   Set the mixer to low speed and slowly pour the melted butter into the mixer. When the butter has been incorporated, add the vanilla and beat until incorporated.

4   Place the madeleine batter mixture into two piping bags. Place the bags in the refrigerator until the batter is set, about 2 hours.

5   Coat your madeleine pans with nonstick cooking spray. Cut a ½-inch slit in the piping bags and pipe about 1 tablespoon of batter in the center of each seashell mold.

6   Place the pans in the oven and bake until the edges of the madeleines turn golden brown, about 10 minutes. Remove from the oven, turn the cookies immediately out onto a cooling rack, and let them cool completely.

7   Once cool, lightly dust the tops of the madeleines with confectioners' sugar and enjoy.

PAIRS WELL WITH: BRUNCH & DESSERT BOARDS

HONEY NUT
Truffles

YIELD: 16 TRUFFLES / **ACTIVE TIME:** 10 MINUTES / **TOTAL TIME**: 2 HOURS

INGREDIENTS

½ cup peanut butter

¼ cup honey

¼ teaspoon kosher salt

1 cup chopped high-quality chocolate

1   Place the peanut butter, honey, and salt in a bowl and stir until well combined. Form teaspoons of the mixture into balls, place them on a parchment-lined baking sheet, and refrigerate for 1 hour.

2   Remove the baking sheet from the refrigerator. Bring water to a simmer in a medium saucepan and place the chocolate in a heatproof mixing bowl. Place the bowl over the simmering water and stir the chocolate occasionally until it is melted.

3   Dip the balls into the melted chocolate until completely coated. Place them back on the baking sheet. When all the truffles have been coated, place them in the refrigerator and chill until the chocolate is set.

PAIRS WELL WITH: NUTS, BRUNCH & DESSERT BOARDS

MERINGUE
Kisses

YIELD: 50 KISSES / **ACTIVE TIME:** 30 MINUTES / **TOTAL TIME:** 1 HOUR AND 30 MINUTES

INGREDIENTS

4 egg whites

7 oz. sugar

Pinch of kosher salt

1 to 2 drops of gel food coloring (optional)

1 teaspoon pure vanilla extract (optional)

1 Preheat the oven to 200°F and line two baking sheets with parchment paper.

2 Fill a small saucepan halfway with water and bring it to a gentle simmer. In the work bowl of a stand mixer, combine the egg whites, sugar, and salt. Place the work bowl over the simmering water and whisk continually until the sugar has dissolved. Remove the bowl from heat and return it to the stand mixer.

3 Fit the mixer with the whisk attachment and whip the mixture on high until it holds stiff peaks. If using coloring or vanilla, add it now and whisk to incorporate.

4 Transfer the meringue to a piping bag fit with a round tip.

5 Pipe the meringue onto the baking sheets, leaving about 1 inch between them. Place the sheets in the oven and bake the meringues until they can be pulled off the parchment cleanly and are no longer sticky in the center, about 1 hour. If the meringues need a little longer, crack the oven door and continue cooking. This will prevent the meringues from browning.

6 Remove from the oven and enjoy immediately.

PAIRS WELL WITH: DESSERT & SPRING-THEMED BOARDS

GRILLED
Pineapple

YIELD: 4 SERVINGS / **ACTIVE TIME:** 15 MINUTES / **TOTAL TIME:** 1 HOUR

INGREDIENTS

1 pineapple, trimmed and peeled

¼ cup honey

¼ cup brown sugar

½ cup water

Zest and juice of 1 lime

1   Preheat a gas or charcoal grill to medium-high heat (about 450°F). Slice the pineapple into rings that are approximately ½ inch thick and remove the center core.

2   Place the pineapple rings on the grill and grill until they are charred nicely on both sides, about 6 minutes. Remove from the grill and transfer the pineapple to a baking dish.

3   Combine the honey, brown sugar, water, lime zest, and lime juice in a saucepan and bring it to a boil over medium heat, stirring to dissolve the brown sugar.

4   Pour the syrup over the pineapple rings and let them marinate for 30 minutes before serving.

PAIRS WELL WITH: CURED MEATS, SPICY FOODS, SUMMER-THEMED BOARDS

HONEYCOMB
Candy

YIELD: 4 SERVINGS / ACTIVE TIME: 15 MINUTES / TOTAL TIME: 1 HOUR

INGREDIENTS

1 cup sugar

¼ cup light corn syrup

2 tablespoons honey

½ cup water

2 teaspoons baking soda

1 Line a square, 8-inch baking dish with parchment paper. Place the sugar, corn syrup, honey, and water in a medium saucepan fitted with a candy thermometer and cook over medium heat, stirring occasionally, until the mixture comes to a boil. Continue to cook, without stirring, until the mixture is 300°F and is light amber in color.

2 Remove the pan from heat and carefully and quickly stir in the baking soda. Pour the mixture into the baking dish, place it in the refrigerator, and chill for at least 45 minutes.

3 Break the mixture into bite-size pieces and serve.

PAIRS WELL WITH: MILD & CREAMY CHEESES, CHERRIES, GAME MEATS

CHOCOLATE-DIPPED
Strawberries

YIELD: 8 SERVINGS / **ACTIVE TIME:** 10 MINUTES / **TOTAL TIME:** 2 HOURS AND 10 MINUTES

INGREDIENTS

2 pints of fresh strawberries

2 cups dark chocolate chips

1 Rinse the strawberries well and pat them dry.

2 Fill a small saucepan halfway with water and bring it to a simmer. Place the chocolate chips in a heatproof bowl and place it over the simmering water. Stir occasionally until the chocolate is melted.

3 Line a baking sheet with parchment paper. Dip each strawberry into the chocolate halfway, or completely, whichever you prefer, and place the strawberries on the sheet. Place in the refrigerator and chill for at least 2 hours before serving.

PAIRS WELL WITH: BRUNCH BOARDS, SMOKED MEATS, NUTS

CANDIED
Bacon

YIELD: 8 SERVINGS / **ACTIVE TIME:** 10 MINUTES / **TOTAL TIME:** 40 MINUTES

INGREDIENTS

1 lb. thick-cut bacon

1 cup brown sugar

1 tablespoon black pepper

1   Preheat the oven to 375°F. Place a wire rack in a rimmed baking sheet and place the bacon on the rack. Sprinkle the brown sugar over the bacon and gently pat it down with your fingers.

2   Sprinkle the pepper over the bacon, place the pan in the oven, and bake the bacon until the sugar has caramelized, about 25 minutes. Remove from the oven and serve warm or at room temperature.

PAIRS WELL WITH: FRUIT, NUTS, BRUNCH BOARDS

ORANGE & ROSEMARY
Shortbread

YIELD: 24 COOKIES / **ACTIVE TIME:** 20 MINUTES / **TOTAL TIME:** 2 HOURS

INGREDIENTS

1 lb. unsalted butter, softened

¼ cup sugar

¼ cup orange juice

1 tablespoon orange zest

2 teaspoons finely chopped fresh rosemary

4½ cups all-purpose flour

Confectioners' sugar, to taste

1 Place all the ingredients, except for the flour and confectioners' sugar, in the work bowl of a stand mixer fitted with the paddle attachment and beat at low speed until the mixture is smooth and creamy.

2 Slowly add the flour and beat until a crumbly dough forms. Press the dough into a rectangle that is approximately ½ inch thick. Cover with plastic wrap and place the dough in the refrigerator for 1 hour.

3 Preheat the oven to 350°F and line two baking sheets with parchment paper. Cut the dough into rounds and place them on the baking sheets. Sprinkle with confectioners' sugar, place in the oven, and bake until the edges start to brown, about 15 minutes.

4 Remove the cookies from the oven and let them cool before serving.

PAIRS WELL WITH: BRUNCH & SPRING-THEMED BOARDS

DARK CHOCOLATE &
Stout Brownies

YIELD: 16 BROWNIES / **ACTIVE TIME:** 15 MINUTES / **TOTAL TIME:** 1 HOUR AND 15 MINUTES

INGREDIENTS

8 oz. unsalted butter, plus more as needed

12 oz. Guinness

12 oz. dark chocolate chips

1½ cups sugar

3 large eggs

1 teaspoon pure vanilla extract

¾ cup all-purpose flour

1¼ teaspoons kosher salt

Cocoa powder, as needed

1 Preheat the oven to 350°F and coat a square 8-inch cake pan with butter. Place the Guinness in a saucepan and bring to a boil. Cook until it has reduced by half. Remove the pan from heat and let it cool.

2 Bring water to a boil in a saucepan. Place the chocolate chips and the butter in a heatproof bowl, place it over the simmering water, and stir until the mixture is smooth.

3 Place the sugar, eggs, and vanilla in a large bowl and stir until combined. Slowly whisk in the chocolate-and-butter mixture and then whisk in the stout.

4 Add the flour and salt and fold to incorporate. Pour batter into the greased pan, place in the oven, and bake for 35 to 40 minutes, until the surface begins to crack and a toothpick inserted into the center comes out with a just few moist crumbs attached.

5 Remove the brownies from the oven, place the pan on a wire rack, and let cool for at least 20 minutes. When cool, sprinkle the cocoa powder over the top and cut the brownies into squares.

PAIRS WELL WITH: DESSERT & FOOTBALL TAILGATE-THEMED BOARDS, FRUIT, GAME MEATS

BLUEBERRY
Buckle

YIELD: 8 TO 10 SERVINGS / **ACTIVE TIME:** 20 MINUTES / **TOTAL TIME:** 2 HOURS

INGREDIENTS

2 cups all-purpose flour

¾ cup sugar

½ cup packed light brown sugar

¼ teaspoon cinnamon

¾ teaspoon kosher salt

14 tablespoons unsalted butter, cut into small pieces and softened

1½ teaspoons baking powder

½ teaspoon lemon zest

1½ teaspoons pure vanilla extract

2 large eggs, at room temperature

1 quart of fresh blueberries

1 Preheat the oven to 350°F and coat a square 8-inch cake pan with nonstick cooking spray. Place ½ cup of the flour, 2 tablespoons of the granulated sugar, the brown sugar, cinnamon, and a pinch of the salt in a mixing bowl and mix until combined. Add 4 tablespoons of the butter and work the mixture with a pastry blender until it resembles wet sand. Set aside.

2 Place the remaining flour and the baking powder in a small bowl and whisk to combine.

3 Place the remaining butter, sugar, and salt, and the lemon zest in the work bowl of a stand mixer fitted with the paddle attachment and beat until the mixture is light and fluffy. Add the vanilla, beat until incorporated, and then add the eggs one at a time. Beat until incorporated and then gradually add the flour mixture. Beat until it has been incorporated. Add the blueberries and then fold the batter until the blueberries have been evenly distributed. Scrape down the work bowl as needed while mixing the batter.

4 Transfer the batter to the cake pan and smooth the surface with a rubber spatula. Sprinkle the sugar-and-cinnamon mixture over the batter, place the cake in the oven, and bake until the top is golden brown and a toothpick inserted into the center comes out clean, about 50 minutes. Remove from the oven and let cool in the pan for 15 minutes.

5 Remove from the pan, transfer to a wire rack, and let cool to room temperature before serving.

PAIRS WELL WITH: BREAKFAST & BRUNCH BOARDS, SMOKED MEATS

PASTRY CREAM

Place 2 cups milk and 1 tablespoon unsalted butter in a saucepan and bring to a simmer over medium heat. Place ½ cup sugar and 3 tablespoons cornstarch in a small bowl and whisk to combine. Add 2 large eggs and whisk until the mixture is smooth and creamy. While stirring constantly, gradually incorporate half of the milk mixture into the egg mixture. Add a pinch of kosher salt and ½ teaspoon of pure vanilla extract, stir to incorporate, and pour the tempered eggs into the saucepan. Cook, stirring constantly, until the mixture is thick enough to coat the back of a wooden spoon, making sure not to let it come to a boil. Pour the cream into a bowl, place plastic wrap directly on the surface to prevent a skin from forming, and refrigerate until cool.

ECLAIRS

YIELD: 12 ECLAIRS / **ACTIVE TIME:** 40 MINUTES / **TOTAL TIME:** 1 HOUR AND 30 MINUTES

INGREDIENTS

17 oz. water

8½ oz. unsalted butter

1 teaspoon fine sea salt

2.4 oz. sugar

12½ oz. all-purpose flour

6 eggs

Pastry Cream (see sidebar)

Chocolate Ganache (see page 393), warm

1 Preheat the oven to 425°F and line two baking sheets with parchment paper. In a medium saucepan, combine the water, butter, salt, and sugar and warm the mixture over medium heat until the butter is melted.

2 Add the flour to the pan and use a rubber spatula or a wooden spoon to fold the mixture until it comes together as a thick, shiny dough, taking care not to let the dough burn.

3 Transfer the dough to the work bowl of a stand mixer fitted with the paddle attachment and beat on medium speed until the dough is no longer steaming and the bowl is just warm to the touch, at least 10 minutes.

4 Incorporate the eggs two at a time, scraping down the work bowl between each addition. Transfer the dough to a piping bag fit with a plain tip. Pipe 12 eclairs onto the baking sheets, leaving 1½ inches between them. They should be approximately 5 inches long.

5 Place the eclairs in the oven and bake for 10 minutes. Lower the oven's temperature to 325°F and bake until golden brown and a cake tester inserted into their centers comes out clean, 20 to 25 minutes. Remove from the oven and let them cool on a wire rack.

6 Fill a piping bag fitted with a plain tip with the Pastry Cream.

7 Using a paring knife, cut 3 small slits on the undersides of the eclairs and fill them with the Pastry Cream.

8 Carefully dip the top halves of the eclairs in the ganache, or drizzle the ganache over the pastries. Allow the chocolate to set before serving.

PAIRS WELL WITH: BRUNCH & DESSERT BOARDS

BAKED

Apples

YIELD: 6 SERVINGS / **ACTIVE TIME:** 15 MINUTES / **TOTAL TIME:** 1 HOUR

INGREDIENTS

6 apples

3 tablespoons unsalted butter, melted

6 tablespoons blackberry jam

2 oz. goat cheese, cut into 6 rounds

1 Preheat the oven to 350°F. Slice the tops off the apples and set them aside. Use a paring knife to cut a circle around the apples' cores and then scoop out their centers. Make sure to leave a ½-inch-thick wall inside each apple.

2 Rub the insides and outsides of the apples with some of the melted butter. Place the jam and goat cheese in a mixing bowl and stir to combine. Fill the apples' cavities with the mixture, place the tops back on the apples, and set them aside.

3 Coat a baking dish with the remaining butter, place the apples in the dish, and place in the oven. Bake until the apples are tender, 25 to 30 minutes. Remove from the oven and let cool briefly before serving.

PAIRS WELL WITH: AUTUMN-THEMED BOARDS, CURED MEATS, PICKLED VEGETABLES

BEIGNETS

YIELD: 15 BEIGNETS / **ACTIVE TIME:** 1 HOUR / **TOTAL TIME:** 24 HOURS

INGREDIENTS

1½ cups milk

2 eggs

2 egg yolks

½ cup sugar

4 oz. unsalted butter, melted

2 tablespoons active dry yeast

25 oz. all-purpose flour,
plus more as needed

1¼ teaspoons kosher salt

4 cups vegetable oil

1 cup confectioners' sugar,
for dusting

1   In the work bowl of a stand mixer fitted with the paddle attachment, combine the milk, eggs, egg yolks, sugar, and butter and beat on medium speed for 2 minutes.

2   Add the yeast, flour, and salt and beat until the mixture comes together as a dough, about 5 minutes.

3   Coat a medium heatproof bowl with nonstick cooking spray, transfer the dough to the bowl, and cover with plastic wrap. Refrigerate overnight.

4   Place the vegetable oil in a Dutch oven fitted with a candy thermometer and warm the oil to 350°F over medium heat. Set a paper towel–lined baking sheet beside the stove.

5   Remove the dough from the refrigerator and place it on a flour-dusted work surface. Roll the dough out until it is ½ inch thick. Cut the dough into 2-inch squares.

6   Working in batches, carefully place the beignets in the oil and fry, turning them once, until browned and cooked through, 2 minutes. Transfer the cooked doughnuts to the baking sheet to drain and cool.

7   When the beignets have cooled, dust them generously with confectioners' sugar and enjoy.

PAIRS WELL WITH: BRUNCH & DESSERT BOARDS

SUFGANIYOT

YIELD: 20 SUFGANIYOT / ACTIVE TIME: 45 MINUTES / TOTAL TIME: 3 HOURS

INGREDIENTS

3½ tablespoons unsalted butter, chopped, plus more as needed

3½ cups all-purpose flour, plus more as needed

½ teaspoon fine sea salt

¼ cup sugar

1 tablespoon instant yeast

1 egg

1¼ cups lukewarm milk (85°F)

Avocado oil, as needed

½ cup strawberry or raspberry jam

¼ cup confectioners' sugar

1 Coat a mixing bowl with some butter and set it aside. Sift the flour into the work bowl of a stand mixer fitted with the dough hook. Add the salt, sugar, and yeast and stir to incorporate.

2 Add the egg and butter to the mixture and mix to incorporate. Gradually add the milk and work the mixture until it comes together as a soft dough, 8 to 10 minutes.

3 Form the dough into a ball and place it in the greased mixing bowl. Cover with a linen towel and let it rise until doubled in size, about 2 hours.

4 Line two baking sheets with parchment paper. Place the dough on a flour-dusted work surface and roll it out until it is about ¾ inch thick. Cut the dough into 2-inch circles, place them on the baking sheets, and cover with a linen towel. Let them rise for another 20 minutes.

5 Add avocado oil to a Dutch oven until it is about 2 inches deep and warm it to 325°F. Add the dough in batches of 4 and fry until golden brown, about 6 minutes, turning them over halfway through.

6 Drain the sufganiyot on a paper towel–lined plate. Fill a piping bag with the jam, and make a small slit on the top of each sufganiyah. Place the piping bag in the slit and fill until you see the filling coming back out. Sprinkle with confectioners' sugar and enjoy.

PAIRS WELL WITH: BREAKFAST, BRUNCH & HOLIDAY-THEMED BOARDS

METRIC CONVERSIONS

U.S. Measurement	Approximate Metric Liquid Measurement	Approximate Metric Dry Measurement
1 teaspoon	5 ml	5 g
1 tablespoon or ½ ounce	15 ml	14 g
1 ounce or ⅛ cup	30 ml	29 g
¼ cup or 2 ounces	60 ml	57 g
⅓ cup	80 ml	76 g
½ cup or 4 ounces	120 ml	113 g
⅔ cup	160 ml	151 g
¾ cup or 6 ounces	180 ml	170 g
1 cup or 8 ounces or ½ pint	240 ml	227 g
1½ cups or 12 ounces	350 ml	340 g
2 cups or 1 pint or 16 ounces	475 ml	454 g
3 cups or 1½ pints	700 ml	680 g
4 cups or 2 pints or 1 quart	950 ml	908 g

INDEX

A

adobo
    Shrimp in Adobo, 224
    Southwestern Sliders, 193
Aguachile Verde, 229
almond flour
    Macarons, 391–392
    Madeleines, 412
almonds
    Empanadas, 242
    Lemon & Almond Biscotti, 408
    Polvorones, 402
    Smoky & Spicy Almonds, 278
amchoor powder
    Punjabi Samosas, 274–275
anchovy fillets
    Bagna Cauda, 110
    Zucchini Sott'olio, 306
apples
    Baked Apples, 432
    Cranberry Relish, 143
    Pickled Applesauce, 175
apricots
    Apricot & Chili Jam, 96
    Baked Brie, Two Ways, 254
    Chicken Sausage, 201
    Mostarda, 112
Arancini, 249
artichoke/artichoke hearts
    Baked Brie, Two Ways, 254
    Fried Artichokes, 372–373
    Roasted Artichoke & Spinach Dip,
      150
Asiago cheese
    Cheesy Poofs, 277
    Stuffed Mushrooms, 361
    Thyme & Asiago Crackers, 53
avocados
    Aguachile Verde, 229
    Guacamole, 114
    Keftes de Espinaca, 376
    Pickled Avocado, 343
    Sweet Corn & Pepita Guacamole, 115

B

Baba Ghanoush, 179
bacon
Bacon Jam, 131
    Candied Bacon, 423
Bagel Chips, 76
Bagna Cauda, 110
Baguettes
    Crostini, 51
    recipe, 24
Baked Apples, 432
Baked Brie, Two Ways, 254
Baked Camembert, 295
Balsamic Ranch, 126
Banana Bread, Rum & Caramelized, 66
basil
    Blueberry & Basil Jam, 105
    Feta & Herb Quickbread, 14
    Pesto, 154
beans
    Falafel, 337
    Hummus, 170
    White Bean & Rosemary Spread, 157
beef
    Beef Carpaccio, 199
    Beef Tataki, 207
    Cornish Pasties, 273
    Kefta, 221
    Papas Rellenas, 270
    Southwestern Sliders, 193
beer
    Beer Cheese, 146
    Dark Chocolate & Stout Brownies,
      427
    Salsa Borracha, 122
beets
    Beet Relish, 166
    Beet-Cured Salmon, 231
Beignets, 435
Black Sesame Sourdough Bread, 20
Blistered Shishito Peppers, 358
blue cheese
    Green Goddess Dip, 153
    Pecan & Blue Cheese Crackers, 61
    Stuffed Prunes, 348
Blue Pea Flower Sourdough Bread, 23
blueberries
    Blueberry & Basil Jam, 105
    Blueberry Buckle, 428
Bread & Butter Pickles, 324

breads and crackers
    Bagel Chips, 76
    Baguettes, 24
    Black Sesame Sourdough Bread, 20
    Blue Pea Flower Sourdough Bread, 23
    Brioche, 31
    Brown Bread, 39
    Bulkie Rolls, 38
    Candied Ritz Crackers, 58
    Challah, 32–33
    Cheese Twists, 82
    Chia Seed Crackers, 60
    Chocolate Cherry Crackers, 65
    Ciabatta, 26
    Crostini, 51
    English Muffins, 67
    Everything Bagels, 90
    Feta & Herb Quickbread, 14
    Fett'unta, 48
    Focaccia, 27
    Fougasse, 36
    Grissini Sticks, 43
    Harvest Loaf, 35
    Honey Cornbread, 71
    Laffa, 86
    Lavash, 64
    Nori Crackers, 78
    Pão de Queijo, 42
    Paratha, 81
    Pecan & Blue Cheese Crackers, 61
    Pita Bread, 85
    Rum & Caramelized Banana Bread,
      66
    Saltines, 72
    Soft Pretzels, 77
    Sourdough Bread, 17
    Sourdough Crackers, 89
    Sourdough Starter, 16
    Stout Gingerbread, 73
    Thyme & Asiago Crackers, 53
    Toast Points, 52
    Whole Wheat Crackers, 47
    Yogurt & Buckwheat Crackers, 57
Brie, Two Ways, Baked, 254
Brioche, 31
Brown Bread, 39
Brussels Sprouts, Fried, 316

Buckwheat Crackers, Yogurt &, 57
bulgur wheat
    Tabbouleh, 165
Bulkie Rolls, 38
buttercreams
    Raspberry Buttercream, 392
    Vanilla Buttercream, 392
buttermilk
    Balsamic Ranch, 126
    Buttermilk Waffles, 266
butters
    Cultured Butter, 106
    Whipped Herb Butter, 101

C

Camembert, Baked, 295
Candied Bacon, 423
Candied Ritz Crackers, 58
canning, about, 325
Cantaloupe Pops, Prosciutto &, 204
Caponata, 304
Caprese Salad, 312
carrots
    Charred Escabeche, 344
cashews
    Dudhi Kofta, 323
    Sicilian Bar Nuts, 259
celery
    Caponata, 304
    White Bean & Rosemary Spread, 157
Challah, 32–33
Charred Escabeche, 344
Charred Octopus, 234
cheddar cheese
    Beer Cheese, 146
cheese
    Cheese Twists, 82
    Cheesy Poofs, 277
    See also individual cheese types
cherries, dried
    Baked Brie, Two Ways, 254
    Chocolate Cherry Crackers, 65
    Mostarda, 112
Chestnuts, Roasted, 253
chia seeds
    Chia Seed Crackers, 60
    Raspberry & Chia Jam, 142
Chicharron, 194
chicken
    Chicken 65, 218

Chicken Chorizo, 186
Chicken Sausage, 201
Popcorn Chicken, 213
chickpea flour
    Dudhi Kofta, 323
chickpeas
    Falafel, 337
    Hummus, 170
chile peppers. *See* peppers, chile
chipotles in adobo
    Shrimp in Adobo, 224
    Southwestern Sliders, 193
chives
    Crab Dip, 136
    Feta & Herb Quickbread, 14
chocolate
    Chocolate Cherry Crackers, 65
    Chocolate Chip Cookies, 386
    Chocolate-Dipped Strawberries, 420
    Dark Chocolate & Stout Brownies, 427
    Honey Nut Truffles, 415
Chocolate Ganache
    Coconut Macaroons, 397
    Eclairs, 431
    recipe, 392
Chorizo, Chicken, 186
chutneys
    Coconut & Cilantro Chutney, 161
    Sultana & Mango Chutney, 138
Ciabatta, 26
cilantro
    Aguachile Verde, 229
    Cilantro Pesto, 113
    Coconut & Cilantro Chutney, 161
    Falafel, 337
    Guacamole, 114
    Lamb Meatballs, 200
    Salsa Verde, 121
    Smoked Oysters, 225
    Southwestern Sliders, 193
    Sweet Corn & Pepita Guacamole, 115
    Tomato Aguachile, 317
Classic Fondue, 256
Classic Gingerbread Cookies, 401
Classic Sugar Cookies, 389
cocoa powder
    Chocolate Cherry Crackers, 65
    Dark Chocolate & Stout Brownies,

427
coconut
    Coconut & Cilantro Chutney, 161
    Coconut Macaroons, 397
cookies
    Chocolate Chip Cookies, 386
    Classic Gingerbread Cookies, 401
    Classic Sugar Cookies, 389
    Coconut Macaroons, 397
    Lemon & Almond Biscotti, 408
    Macarons, 391–392
    Madeleines, 412
    Orange & Rosemary Shortbread, 424
    Orange Spritz, 398
    Polvorones, 402
    Snickerdoodles, 390
corn
    Corn Fritters, 355
    Sweet Corn & Pepita Guacamole, 115
Corn Dogs, 222
Cornbread, Honey, 71
Cornish Pasties, 273
cornmeal
    Brown Bread, 39
    Corn Dogs, 222
    Honey Cornbread, 71
crab
    Crab Dip, 136
    Crab Rangoon, 245
crackers
    Candied Ritz Crackers, 58
    Chia Seed Crackers, 60
    Chocolate Cherry Crackers, 65
    Nori Crackers, 78
    Pecan & Blue Cheese Crackers, 61
    Saltines, 72
    Sourdough Crackers, 89
    Thyme & Asiago Crackers, 53
    Whole Wheat Crackers, 47
    Yogurt & Buckwheat Crackers, 57
    See also breads and crackers
cranberries
    Cranberry Relish, 143
    Granola, 262
    Harvest Loaf, 35
cream cheese
    Crab Dip, 136
    Crab Rangoon, 245
    Stuffed Mushrooms, 361

Creamy Quark & Mozzarella Dip, 102
Crispy Pancetta, 206
Crostini, 51
cucumbers
    Aguachile Verde, 229
    Bread & Butter Pickles, 324
    Cucumber, Tomato & Mango Relish,
        178
    Tabbouleh, 165
    Tomato Aguachile, 317
    Tzatziki, 128
Cultured Butter, 106
Cured Egg Yolks, 265
Curried Pistachios, 258

D

Dark Chocolate & Stout Brownies, 427
desserts
    Baked Apples, 432
    Beignets, 435
    Blueberry Buckle, 428
    Candied Bacon, 423
    Chocolate Chip Cookies, 386
    Chocolate-Dipped Strawberries, 420
    Classic Gingerbread Cookies, 401
    Classic Sugar Cookies, 389
    Coconut Macaroons, 397
    Dark Chocolate & Stout Brownies,
        427
    Eclairs, 431
    Grilled Pineapple, 418
    Honey Nut Truffles, 415
    Honeycomb Candy, 419
    Lemon & Almond Biscotti, 408
    Lemon Squares, 411
    Macarons, 391–392
    Madeleines, 412
    Meringue Kisses, 416
    Orange & Rosemary Shortbread, 424
    Orange Spritz, 398
    Polvorones, 402
    Snickerdoodles, 390
    Sufganiyot, 436
    Torcetti di Saint Vincent, 407
dill
    Bread & Butter Pickles, 324
    Cucumber, Tomato & Mango Relish,
        178
dips, spreads, and condiments
    Apricot & Chili Jam, 96

Baba Ghanoush, 179
Bacon Jam, 131
Bagna Cauda, 110
Balsamic Ranch, 126
Beer Cheese, 146
Beet Relish, 166
Blueberry & Basil Jam, 105
Cilantro Pesto, 113
Coconut & Cilantro Chutney, 161
Crab Dip, 136
Cranberry Relish, 143
Creamy Quark & Mozzarella Dip, 102
Cucumber, Tomato & Mango Relish,
    178
Cultured Butter, 106
Green Goddess Dip, 153
Green Tomato Jam, 99
Guacamole, 114
Habanero Honey, 123
Hummus, 170
Italian Dipping Oil, 132
Labneh, 180
Mignonette Sauce, 147
Mostarda, 112
Orange Marmalade, 145
Pea & Parmesan Dip, 98
Pecan Muhammara, 169
Pesto, 154
Pickled Applesauce, 175
Pomegranate Reduction, 139
Pork Pâté, 109
Raspberry & Chia Jam, 142
Red Zhug, 174
Roasted Artichoke & Spinach Dip,
    150
Roasted Garlic Aioli, 127
Roasted Pumpkin Dip, 158
Salsa Borracha, 122
Salsa de Chiltomate, 118
Salsa Verde, 121
Smoked Potato Puree, 162
Sultana & Mango Chutney, 138
Sweet Corn & Pepita Guacamole, 115
Tabbouleh, 165
Tequila Cheese Dip, 133
Tzatziki, 128
Whipped Herb Butter, 101
White Bean & Rosemary Spread, 157
Duck Rillette, 212

Dudhi Kofta, 323
dumplings
    Arancini, 249
    Cheesy Poofs, 277
    Cornish Pasties, 273
    Crab Rangoon, 245
    Empanadas, 242
    Papas Rellenas, 270
    Punjabi Samosas, 274–275
    Takoyaki, 246
Duxelles, 349

E

Eclairs, 431
eggplant
    Baba Ghanoush, 179
    Caponata, 304
    Eggplant Rings, 354
    Turkish Eggplant Salad, 371
eggs
    Cured Egg Yolks, 265
    Southern Deviled Eggs, 298
    Spanish Tortilla, 320
Emmental cheese
    Classic Fondue, 256
Empanadas, 242
English Muffins, 67
Everything Bagels
    Bagel Chips, 76
    recipe, 90

F

Falafel, 337
feta cheese
    Feta & Herb Quickbread, 14
    Marinated Feta, 290
    Tabbouleh, 165
    Tiropitakia, 362
Fett'unta, 48
figs/fig spread
    Baked Brie, Two Ways, 254
    Prosciutto-Wrapped Figs, 189
fillings, 392
fish
    Beet-Cured Salmon, 231
    Swordfish Crudo, 236
    See also seafood
Focaccia, 27
Foie Gras Torchon, 195
Fondue, Classic, 256

Fontina cheese
    Arancini, 249
    Cheese Twists, 82
Fougasse, 36
Fried Artichokes, 372–373
Fried Brussels Sprouts, 316
Fried Mustard Greens, 345
Fried Squash Blossoms, 328

G

garlic
    Baba Ghanoush, 179
    Bagna Cauda, 110
    Caponata, 304
    Creamy Quark & Mozzarella Dip, 102
    Falafel, 337
    Hummus, 170
    Italian Dipping Oil, 132
    Marinated Olives, 379
    Peperonata, 311
    Popcorn Chicken, 213
    Red Zhug, 174
    Roasted Artichoke & Spinach Dip, 150
    Roasted Garlic, 315
    Roasted Garlic Aioli, 127
    Salsa Borracha, 122
    Salsa de Chiltomate, 118
    Salsa Verde, 121
    Shrimp in Adobo, 224
    Southwestern Sliders, 193
    Stuffed Mushrooms, 361
    Turkish Eggplant Salad, 371
ginger
    Chicken 65, 218
    Dudhi Kofta, 323
    Green Tomato Jam, 99
    Kachori, 280
    Sultana & Mango Chutney, 138
ginger, crystallized
    Mostarda, 112
ginger, pickled
    Takoyaki, 246
Gingerbread, Stout, 73
goat cheese
    Baked Apples, 432
    Goat Cheese with Herbs, 297
gouda cheese
    Classic Fondue, 256
Granola

Baked Camembert, 295
    recipe, 262
Grapes, Roasted, 307
Green Goddess Dip, 153
Green Tomato Jam, 99
Grilled Halloumi, 287
Grilled Pineapple, 418
Grissini Sticks, 43
Gruyère cheese
    Classic Fondue, 256
Guacamole
    recipe, 114
    Sweet Corn & Pepita Guacamole, 115

H

Habanero Honey, 123
Halloumi, Grilled, 287
Harvest Loaf, 35
Herb Butter, Whipped, 101
honey
    Everything Bagels, 90
    Green Tomato Jam, 99
    Grilled Pineapple, 418
    Habanero Honey, 123
    Honey Cornbread, 71
    Honey Nut Truffles, 415
    Honeycomb Candy, 419
    Raspberry & Chia Jam, 142
hot dogs
    Corn Dogs, 222
Hummus, 170

I

Italian Dipping Oil, 132

J

jack cheese, jalapeño
    Southwestern Sliders, 193
jams
    Apricot & Chili Jam, 96
    Bacon Jam, 131
    Blueberry & Basil Jam, 105
    Green Tomato Jam, 99
    Orange Marmalade, 145
    Raspberry & Chia Jam, 142

K

Kachori, 280
Kale Chips, 366
kefalotyri cheese
    Tiropitakia, 362
Kefta, 221

Keftes de Espinaca, 376

L

Labneh, 180
Laffa, 86
lamb
    Kefta, 221
    Lamb Meatballs, 200
Lavash, 64
Lemon Curd, 392
Lemon Ricotta, 281
lemons
    Fried Artichokes, 372–373
    Lemon & Almond Biscotti, 408
    Lemon Squares, 411
    Okra & Lemons with Za'atar, 381
    Orange Marmalade, 145
lime juice
    Aguachile Verde, 229
    Tequila Cheese Dip, 133
    Tomato Aguachile, 317

M

Macarons, 391–392
Madeleines, 412
maida flour
    Punjabi Samosas, 274–275
mangos/mango jam
    Cucumber, Tomato & Mango Relish, 178
    Sultana & Mango Chutney, 138
maple syrup
    Baked Camembert, 295
    Granola, 262
    Green Tomato Jam, 99
    Maple Walnuts, 250
Marinated Feta, 290
Marinated Mozzarella, 291
Marinated Olives, 379
Masa-Crusted Sardines, 230
Meringue Kisses, 416
mezcal
    Salsa Borracha, 122
Mignonette Sauce, 147
mint
    Coconut & Cilantro Chutney, 161
    Fried Squash Blossoms, 328
    Kefta, 221
    Pea & Parmesan Dip, 98
    Tabbouleh, 165
    Tzatziki, 128

molasses
    Brown Bread, 39
    Classic Gingerbread Cookies, 401
    Stout Gingerbread, 73
mortadella
    Muffuletta, 217
Mostarda, 112
mozzarella cheese
    Caprese Salad, 312
    Cheesy Poofs, 277
    Creamy Quark & Mozzarella Dip, 102
    Marinated Mozzarella, 291
Muffuletta, 217
mushrooms
    Duxelles, 349
    Stuffed Mushrooms, 361
Mustard Greens, Fried, 345

N
Nori Crackers, 78
nuts. *See individual nut types*

O
oats
    Granola, 262
Oaxaca cheese
    Tequila Cheese Dip, 133
octopus
    Charred Octopus, 234
    Takoyaki, 246
Okra & Lemons with Za'atar, 381
olives
    Baked Brie, Two Ways, 254
    Caponata, 304
    Marinated Olives, 379
    Muffuletta, 217
    Papas Rellenas, 270
    Peperonata, 311
    Tapenade, 353
onion
    Arancini, 249
    Bread & Butter Pickles, 324
    Caponata, 304
    Cornish Pasties, 273
    Cucumber, Tomato & Mango Relish, 178
    Dudhi Kofta, 323
    Empanadas, 242
    Falafel, 337
    Keftes de Espinaca, 376
    Lamb Meatballs, 200

Papas Rellenas, 270
Peperonata, 311
Pickled Red Onion, 350
Red Zhug, 174
Spanish Tortilla, 320
Stuffed Mushrooms, 361
Tomato Aguachile, 317
Turkish Eggplant Salad, 371
oranges
    Cranberry Relish, 143
    Orange & Rosemary Shortbread, 424
    Orange Marmalade, 145
    Orange Spritz, 398
    Pickled Rhubarb, 335
Oysters, Smoked, 225

P
Pão de Queijo, 42
Pancetta, Crispy, 206
panko
    Arancini, 249
    Crab Dip, 136
    Eggplant Rings, 354
Papas Rellenas, 270
Paratha, 81
Parmesan cheese
    Cheese Twists, 82
    Cheesy Poofs, 277
    Focaccia, 27
    Fougasse, 36
    Pão de Queijo, 42
    Parmesan Crisps, 285
    Parmesan Spheres, 286
    Pea & Parmesan Dip, 98
    Pesto, 154
    Roasted Pumpkin Dip, 158
    Sicilian Meatballs, 190
parsley
    Duck Rillette, 212
    Falafel, 337
    Kefta, 221
    Lamb Meatballs, 200
    Muffuletta, 217
    Red Zhug, 174
    Tabbouleh, 165
    Tiropitakia, 362
    Turkish Eggplant Salad, 371
parsnips
    Cornish Pasties, 273
Pastry Cream

Eclairs, 431
Pea & Parmesan Dip, 98
peanut butter
    Honey Nut Truffles, 415
peas
    Kachori, 280
pecans
    Baked Brie, Two Ways, 254
    Granola, 262
    Pecan & Blue Cheese Crackers, 61
    Pecan Muhammara, 169
    Sicilian Bar Nuts, 259
Peperonata, 311
peppers, bell
    Caponata, 304
    Muffuletta, 217
    Papas Rellenas, 270
    Pecan Muhammara, 169
    Peperonata, 311
peppers, chile
    Aguachile Verde, 229
    Apricot & Chili Jam, 96
    Blistered Shishito Peppers, 358
    Bread & Butter Pickles, 324
    Charred Escabeche, 344
    Chicken 65, 218
    Chicken Chorizo, 186
    Coconut & Cilantro Chutney, 161
    Dudhi Kofta, 323
    Falafel, 337
    Guacamole, 114
    Habanero Honey, 123
    Kachori, 280
    Marinated Olives, 379
    Pecan Muhammara, 169
    Pickled Pineapple, 331
    Red Zhug, 174
    Salsa Borracha, 122
    Salsa de Chiltomate, 118
    Salsa Verde, 121
    Shrimp in Adobo, 224
    Smoked Oysters, 225
    Southwestern Sliders, 193
    Swordfish Crudo, 236
    Tequila Cheese Dip, 133
    Tomato Aguachile, 317
    Vegetarian Taquitos, 330
pestos
    Caprese Salad, 312

Cilantro Pesto, 113
Marinated Mozzarella, 291
Pesto, 154
phyllo dough
Tiropitakia, 362
Pickled Applesauce, 175
Pickled Avocado, 343
Pickled Green Tomatoes, 375
Pickled Pineapple, 331
Pickled Red Onion, 350
Pickled Rhubarb, 335
Pickles, Bread & Butter, 324
pine nuts
Pesto, 154
Sicilian Meatballs, 190
pineapple
Grilled Pineapple, 418
Pickled Pineapple, 331
pistachios
Chicken Sausage, 201
Curried Pistachios, 258
Pita Bread, 85
Plums with Tahini Dressing, Roasted, 380
Polvorones, 402
pomegranate seeds/juice
Baba Ghanoush, 179
Pomegranate Reduction, 139
Sweet Corn & Pepita Guacamole, 115
Popcorn Chicken, 213
pork
Empanadas, 242
Pork Pâté, 109
Sicilian Meatballs, 190
pork belly
Chicharron, 194
portobello mushrooms
Duxelles, 349
potatoes
Cornish Pasties, 273
Keftes de Espinaca, 376
Papas Rellenas, 270
Punjabi Samosas, 274–275
Purple Potato Chips, 327
Smoked Potato Puree, 162
Spanish Tortilla, 320
Pretzels, Soft, 77
prosciutto
Prosciutto & Cantaloupe Pops, 204

Prosciutto-Wrapped Figs, 189
provolone cheese
Muffuletta, 217
Prunes, Stuffed, 348
puff pastry
Cheese Twists, 82
Pumpkin Dip, Roasted, 158
pumpkin seeds
Harvest Loaf, 35
Sweet Corn & Pepita Guacamole, 115
Punjabi Samosas, 274–275
Purple Potato Chips, 327

Q
Quark & Mozzarella Dip, Creamy, 102
queso enchilada
Cilantro Pesto, 113
queso fresco
Fried Squash Blossoms, 328
Tomato Aguachile, 317
quickbreads
Feta & Herb Quickbread, 14
Rum & Caramelized Banana Bread, 66

R
raisins
Brown Bread, 39
Chicken Sausage, 201
Empanadas, 242
Green Tomato Jam, 99
Papas Rellenas, 270
Sultana & Mango Chutney, 138
Raspberry & Chia Jam, 142
Raspberry Buttercream, 392
Red Zhug
Eggplant Rings, 354
recipe, 174
Rhubarb, Pickled, 335
rice
Arancini, 249
ricotta cheese
Lemon Ricotta, 281
Vegetarian Taquitos, 330
Roasted Artichoke & Spinach Dip, 150
Roasted Chestnuts, 253
Roasted Garlic, 315
Roasted Garlic Aioli, 127
Roasted Grapes, 307
Roasted Plums with Tahini Dressing, 380
Roasted Pumpkin Dip, 158

Roasted Tomatoes, 340
rosemary
Orange & Rosemary Shortbread, 424
White Bean & Rosemary Spread, 157
Rum & Caramelized Banana Bread, 66

S
Salmon, Beet-Cured, 231
Salsa Borracha, 122
Salsa de Chiltomate, 118
Salsa Verde, 121
Saltines, 72
Samosas, Punjabi, 274–275
Sardines, Masa-Crusted, 230
sausage
Chicken Chorizo, 186
Chicken Sausage, 201
Sicilian Meatballs, 190
Stuffed Mushrooms, 361
scallions
Falafel, 337
Scallion Pancakes, 365
Tabbouleh, 165
Takoyaki, 246
seafood
Aguachile Verde, 229
Beet-Cured Salmon, 231
Charred Octopus, 234
Crab Dip, 136
Crab Rangoon, 245
Masa-Crusted Sardines, 230
Shrimp Cocktail, 237
Shrimp in Adobo, 224
Smoked Oysters, 225
Swordfish Crudo, 236
sesame seeds
Black Sesame Sourdough Bread, 20
Nori Crackers, 78
shallots
Beet Relish, 166
Crab Dip, 136
Duxelles, 349
Mignonette Sauce, 147
Mostarda, 112
Shishito Peppers, Blistered, 358
shrimp
Aguachile Verde, 229
Shrimp Cocktail, 237
Shrimp in Adobo, 224
Sicilian Bar Nuts, 259

Sicilian Meatballs, 190
Smoked Oysters, 225
Smoked Potato Puree, 162
Smoky & Spicy Almonds, 278
Snickerdoodles, 390
Soft Pretzels, 77
soppressata
    Muffuletta, 217
Sourdough Bread, 17
Sourdough Crackers, 89
Sourdough Starter
    Baguettes, 24
    Black Sesame Sourdough Bread, 20
    Blue Pea Flower Sourdough Bread, 23
    recipe, 16
    Sourdough Bread, 17
    Sourdough Crackers, 89
Southern Deviled Eggs, 298
Southwestern Sliders, 193
Spam
    Southern Deviled Eggs, 298
Spanish Tortilla, 320
spinach
    Creamy Quark & Mozzarella Dip, 102
    Keftes de Espinaca, 376
    Pesto, 154
    Roasted Artichoke & Spinach Dip,
    150
squash, summer
    Creamy Quark & Mozzarella Dip, 102
    Dudhi Kofta, 323
    Zucchini Sott'olio, 306
Squash Blossoms, Fried, 328
stout
    Dark Chocolate & Stout Brownies,
    427
    Stout Gingerbread, 73
strawberries
    Chocolate-Dipped Strawberries, 420
    Strawberry Chips, 336
Stuffed Mushrooms, 361
Stuffed Prunes, 348
Sufganiyot, 436
Sultana & Mango Chutney, 138
summer squash
    Creamy Quark & Mozzarella Dip, 102
    Dudhi Kofta, 323
    Zucchini Sott'olio, 306
sun-dried tomatoes

Muffuletta, 217
Tapenade, 353
sunflower seeds
    Chocolate Cherry Crackers, 65
    Cilantro Pesto, 113
Sweet Corn & Pepita Guacamole, 115
sweet potatoes
    Cheesy Poofs, 277
    Smoked Potato Puree, 162
Swiss chard
    Creamy Quark & Mozzarella Dip, 102
Swordfish Crudo, 236

T

Tabbouleh, 165
tahini
    Baba Ghanoush, 179
    Black Sesame Sourdough Bread, 20
    Hummus, 170
    Roasted Plums with Tahini Dressing,
    380
Takoyaki, 246
Tapenade, 353
tapioca starch
    Pão de Queijo, 42
    Popcorn Chicken, 213
tequila
    Salsa Borracha, 122
    Tequila Cheese Dip, 133
Thyme & Asiago Crackers, 53
Tiropitakia, 362
Toast Points, 52
tomatillos
    Salsa Borracha, 122
    Salsa Verde, 121
tomatoes
    Baked Brie, Two Ways, 254
    Caponata, 304
    Caprese Salad, 312
    Coconut & Cilantro Chutney, 161
    Cucumber, Tomato & Mango Relish,
    178
    Empanadas, 242
    Green Tomato Jam, 99
    Guacamole, 114
    Pickled Green Tomatoes, 375
    Roasted Tomatoes, 340
    Salsa de Chiltomate, 118
    Shrimp in Adobo, 224
    Swordfish Crudo, 236

Tabbouleh, 165
Tequila Cheese Dip, 133
Tomato Aguachile, 317
Turkish Eggplant Salad, 371
See also sun-dried tomatoes
Torcetti di Saint Vincent, 407
tortillas
    Vegetarian Taquitos, 330
Turkish Eggplant Salad, 371
turnips
    Cornish Pasties, 273
Tzatziki, 128

V

Vanilla Buttercream, 392
Vegetarian Taquitos, 330
Venison Jerky, 211

W

Waffles, Buttermilk, 266
walnuts
    Maple Walnuts, 250
    Sicilian Bar Nuts, 259
Whipped Herb Butter, 101
White Bean & Rosemary Spread, 157
Whole Wheat Crackers, 47
wine, red
    Pickled Red Onion, 350
    Pickled Rhubarb, 335
wine, white
    Arancini, 249
    Classic Fondue, 256
    Mostarda, 112

Y

yogurt
    Chicken 65, 218
    Cultured Butter, 106
    Feta & Herb Quickbread, 14
    Labneh, 180
    Roasted Pumpkin Dip, 158
    Tzatziki, 128
    Yogurt & Buckwheat Crackers, 57

Z

zucchini
    Dudhi Kofta, 323
    Zucchini Sott'olio, 306
    See also summer squash

ABOUT CIDER MILL PRESS BOOK PUBLISHERS

Good ideas ripen with time. From seed to harvest, Cider Mill Press brings fine reading, information, and entertainment together between the covers of its creatively crafted books. Our Cider Mill bears fruit twice a year, publishing a new crop of titles each spring and fall.

"Where Good Books Are Ready for Press"
501 Nelson Place
Nashville, Tennessee 37214

cidermillpress.com